SHELBY AND ME
OUR JOURNEY THROUGH LIFE BOOKS

created and written by Donna H. Foster

illustrations and design by Maya Preisler

Wagging Tales Publishers, L.L.C.

ISBN: 978-0-578-51381-2

For more information
visit www.ShelbyandMe.com.

To contact the author, email donnafoster@shelbyandme.com
To contact the illustrator, email mayapreisler@gmail.com

CONTENTS

From the Author 3
Introduction 4
Shelby and Me: Our Journey Through Life Books 8
How to Share Our Life Stories 9
Shelby's Story Begins.. 10
Coming into Foster Care 15
My Dirst Day in My Foster Home 16
Meeting Bear 18
Where Do I Sleep?... 21
Where and What Do I Eat? 23
Where and When Can I Use the Bathroom? 25
Bear's and My Favorite Place 26
Meeting Sassy the Cat.. 28
Missing My Birth Family 32
Visits with Birth Parents 36
Can I Show My Real Feelings? 38
Jumping Jack Goes Home: Reunification 44
Growing Up with Another Family: Adoption 48
Moving into My Adoptive Home 55
My First Day in My Adoptive Home... 57
Toby's Story: Physical Abuse 61
Life with the Family I Adopted.. 67
We Adopt Bac Mookie: International Adoption................................ 69
When a Friend is Gone: Grieving 75
Learning Who I Am... 79
Tracking Down My History 81
Shelby's Life Book Examples 86
Shelby and Me: My Life Book 93

FROM THE AUTHOR

I was gifted seventeen years as a foster parent and more than thirty-two years in the field as a state and national trainer, author and humorous motivational speaker. This has given me the knowledge and experience to be familiar with children's needs in foster care, with children being reunited with birth families and with children being adopted. All of the wonderful people I have met in this field have been a huge part of my learning. My most important teachers are the children who lived with me and have honored me with their stories of strength. God took my life one step further, inspiring me to create a different kind of life book. Hopefully, this life book series gives children a voice and excites them to tell their own stories.

Many life experiences have prepared me for this life book journey. I am a birth parent of two children. Later in life, I became blessed with three stepchildren, sons and daughters-in-law. I am enjoying my later years as a grandmother and great-grandmother.

I want to thank my husband, Tony, for not letting me drift from this goal. Family and friends encouraged me and held me accountable. Social workers, co-workers, therapists, foster parents, and adoptive parents were excited to have a tool like this to help children who have been traumatized. All of this was the confirmation I needed to complete this book and the children's life book pages. I am thankful the Lord trusted me with His vision. I am so thankful for every word of guidance and encouragement.

"Ask, and it shall be given you; seek, and ye shall find; knock, and it shall be opened unto you."
Luke 11:9

KEYNOTES AND WORKSHOPS

Donna Foster is nationally known for her humorous keynotes and workshops. She uses her personal experiences as a foster parent and birth parent to help participants feel safe to discuss serious subjects. She effortlessly engages group participation in enhancing a stress-free learning atmosphere. Her experience as a trainer began in 1982 and still, her contagious energy motivates her audiences. Along with her other contracts, she is a Trainer and Consultant in Staff Development of North Carolina Department of Health and Human Services for 21 years.

Articles in www.fosteringperspectives.org

Contact: donnafoster@shelbyandme.com

INTRODUCTION

"Shelby and Me" is a unique spin on life books. Children who enter the Social Service system have been traumatized and may have difficulty holding on to a positive self-concept. Moving into foster care is just one of the many traumas children experience. Being confused, they have many questions about their lives. Because adults in their past have hurt or neglected them, they have trouble trusting the adults who are there to protect them. Children tend to trust and share more easily with other children and animals. Realizing this, the main character of this series is a big cuddly dog named Shelby who will befriend the child and capture the child's attention and trust. The title of the life book series is "Shelby and Me." "Shelby" is the dog and "Me" is the child reading this book. Shelby shares her story and asks the child to share their life story using the child's own life book pages. The result is that Shelby excitedly engages the child in creating his or her own life book. "Shelby and Me" is written for readers aged 2nd through 5th grade. Younger children will enjoy having this book read to them.

- Shelby, a golden retriever dog, shares her experiences of losing her birth parents, living in foster care and of being adopted.
- The story is written in "first person" or should I say "first dog."
- Children will be able to relate to Shelby through her three homes and how traumatic it is to move. She discloses her feelings of missing her birth family and adjusting to her foster family. She remembers how the people in her life helped her transition from her birth family home to her foster home and lastly to her adoptive home.
- Shelby will make children laugh at her silly antics and love her sweet personality. Shelby talks about how she made friends with people and other animals.
- Shelby reveals all of the questions she had when she came into foster care. These questions include: why she came into foster care, what she could do or not do in the foster home, and how to communicate within this family. These questions repeated themselves when she was adopted into another family.
- Grieving is discussed, and ways to get help working through the many mixed emotions are explored. Shelby constantly mentions missing her birth family and the life she left. She also feels the love and compassion of the people and animals around her who really care for her.
- Children connect with Shelby because they experience many of the same feelings. Shelby guides the child through life changes, such as keeping the connections with birth family. She shows how Shared Parenting helps strengthen all of the connections between birth family, foster family and adopted family.
- In language the child can understand, Shelby teaches the child the differences between foster care, reunification with birth family, and adoption.

THE CHILD'S LIFE BOOK PAGES

After each section, Shelby gives the similarities and differences between children and animals, such as how children come into foster care. *Information for Children* is in *bold italics*. Suggested questions are given to children to ask their birth parents, foster parents, adoptive parents, social workers, or other team members.

- Life book pages are for the child to complete and add to their own life book binders. Life book pages are about the child and include the many questions children may have with spaces for the answers. Other information can include their identification, likes and dislikes, talents, skills, friends, memory pages, collections and more. Life books are an on-going journey. When one life book binder is full, they can create another one and continue this process.
- As Shelby tells her story, learning points are given to the children's caregivers and team members. As an example, Shelby talks about missing her old brown shoe from her birth family barn. She loved to chew on that old brown shoe and she always slept with it. She left her old brown shoe behind when she came into foster care. A little girl in the foster home tenderly gave her a stuffed bear to help Shelby sleep. Shelby appreciated the stuffed bear but it did not comfort her like her old brown shoe comforted her. The learning point is that caregivers need to recognize that the "things" children bring into the foster home are precious to them. Even the smells on the items they bring can comfort the child. It reminds them of "home." Foster parents and adoptive parents can caringly give new things to children but must always realize what the child brings should be honored and respected.
- Shelby will guide the adults in developing the child's life book while entertaining them and the child. It is important that a trusted adult is with the child while reading this book because the child may experience many emotions. Share the child's reactions with the child's social worker and therapist. Enjoy building a special relationship with the child!

HELPFUL HINTS IN USING THIS BOOK:

"Shelby and Me" is a creative way to help a child open up and share their own life story and feelings. This is a time when you can build a closer relationship with the child. This book may open children up to talking about their feelings about their birth family, foster family, and/or adoptive family. Questions the child may have about their life experiences and the answers given can be shared creatively and documented in a personalized approach. Gaps in the child's life can be filled with recalled memories. This life book technique is a fun and therapeutic way for the child's team to come together to build the child's self-esteem and identity. It creates a foundation for helping the child to feel safe, empowered and to celebrate their connections.

- Before reading to child, read the book yourself so you will be familiar with the content.
- Create a quiet uninterrupted "Shelby and Me" time when you and the child can read the book together. It is important that an adult be with the child to talk about their similar experiences with Shelby.
- Read small sections at a time and help the child fill out the corresponding life book pages. Take in consideration the child's developmental age.
- This should be a serious but fun activity that the child shares with you.
- Consider individuals on the team who may want to be a part of helping the child on certain sections of the life book. For example, on a visit with birth parents, the child and birth parent could work on the birth family sections. The social worker can answer questions and share

making life book pages with the child.

- Be prepared for the child to show a range of emotions. All emotions are okay. This is healthy, and it is why uninterrupted time is important. Be open to the child's questions and feelings. Be honest and sensitive with the answers. Children may have been traumatized several times in their young lives. This may be the first time the child will have shared some of the traumatizing events in their lives with anyone.
- Trauma triggers may be discovered. Shelby experienced severe hunger. The first few days in her foster home Shelby didn't trust food would be given to her every day. So when she had a meal there was a trauma trigger for survival and she hid food under her blanket to survive.
- Children want to continue to believe that their birth families love them. They need to hold on to any positive pieces of their lives.
- It is important to share the child's emotional reactions with the social worker. More mental health intervention or support may be needed.
- Suggest that the child share their life book with close team members. It is their book and should be shared with their permission. Their life book follows the child in every move.

SETTING UP A CHILD'S LIFE BOOK:

- Buy a 3-ring notebook with a cover insert. You may want to let the child decorate it with stickers.
- Add page protectors to protect the life book pages.
- Use colored card stock paper for the child's art, photos, collections, etc.
- Have a varied selection of markers, glue, scissors, stickers and other scrap book supplies. Acid-free and lignum-free materials preserves the pages.

SHELBY AND ME
OUR JOURNEY THROUGH LIFE BOOKS
SHELBY

SHELBY AND ME:

OUR JOURNEY THROUGH LIFE BOOKS

Arf---Woof---Arf---Arf! These are dog sounds for "Hi Friend!" My name is Shelby. My person mom tells me I am a beautiful Golden Retriever. I am big, soft and sweet. Can you see my picture? I love to be petted, especially behind my ears.

Will you be my friend? Let's get to know each other. I have a lot of questions to ask you. What is your name? How old are you? Do you have a picture of yourself you can tape or paste on one of the life book pages I have made for you to put in your own life book?

I bet we have a lot in common. Yes, even though I am a dog and you are a boy or girl, we share many of the same kind of experiences. I have lived in different houses with different people and animals. I like a lot of things and I don't like a lot of things. There are things that scare me and things that make me happy. Let's share our life stories. I would love to know more about you. Let's have fun getting to know each other.

HOW TO SHARE OUR LIFE STORIES

Friends, this is how we can share our life stories!

CREATING YOUR LIFE BOOK

- I will share my story through this book. You can share your story, too.
- You can fill out your life book pages. You will find the corresponding life book page number(s) in a box at the bottom of the Shelby and Me pages. You can read my story, then stop and fill out your life book pages, or you can fill out your life book pages during other times. It is up to you.
- Add photos, drawings and stickers to your pages. You can color the Shelby drawings in this book and on your life book pages. Be creative! Your Life Book is yours to keep.
- Put your completed life book pages into "page protectors" to keep them safe in your Life Book binder.
- Keep your inserts and the other stuff you want to keep in a 3—ring binder.
- Using construction paper and glue, add your own art work, poems, journal, other writings, school work and collectibles (movie tickets, magazine pictures, letters, etc).

I am so excited to see what you create in your Life Book!

SHELBY'S STORY BEGINS...

I remember some of my past and how my family's happy life changed. My mommy, daddy, brother, sisters and I lived in a huge brown barn with a giant tree next to it. We loved to take naps under the branches of the tree. It was so cool when the weather was hot. Mr. Farmer, our older person, came out every day to our barn to feed our family plus two horses, four goats, fifteen chickens and four cats. He would pet our heads and talk to us. When I was five months old, Mr. Farmer stopped coming to feed us.

"Mommy, where is Mr. Farmer? We are hungry and I miss him."

Mommy and Daddy did not know why Mr. Farmer stopped coming to feed us. Soon strange people walked into our barn and took away the horses, chickens, cats and goats.

The people talked to each other. "Mr. Farmer is very sick. We need to get all of the animals out of here."

We did not want to leave the barn so we hid in a horse stall behind a big wooden box. We were happy that they did not find us. As the days passed, we realized Mr. Farmer was not coming back. My parents started growling at each other a lot. I found out they were worried about how they were going to feed us. My daddy decided to go outside our "safe barn land" to find food. We waited a long time for daddy to return but he didn't come back. We knew he was lost. We missed him and howled out to him every day.

"Howl!!!!   Howl!!!!!"

My mommy started whimpering because we only had berries to eat.

I cuddled next to her, "Mommy, I will go out and look for food."

She didn't want me to go but I really wanted to help my mommy, brother and sisters. Now being seven months old, I felt big enough to help my family. Seven months is big in dog years.

The next morning I left my barn. It was scary, but I wanted to help my family. I walked alone through the woods. I couldn't find food and had to walk outside of our "safe barn land" to search for some. After walking a very long time, the sun went down and it became very dark. Strange noises made the dark night scary. I had never slept alone so going to sleep was difficult.

As I was closing my eyes, a huge bird with big eyes screamed, "WHOO—WHOO!"

I remember being so scared that I ran and ran! I ran until I fell into some soft grass. I was so tired when I fell. I lay there and drifted off to sleep and dreamed about my barn. I wanted my mommy and daddy.

The bright sun woke me up in the morning. I jumped up and turned around and around looking for my way home. My stomach made hungry sounds. I was scared and lost.

My head hung low as I continued to walk. I howled for my mommy and daddy. "HOWL!!!!" No one howled back.

I kept walking, hoping to find my barn and mommy. Several sun-ups later I stepped on gray, hard, flat ground. A bunch of strange animals with round legs flew past me. They made loud honking noises. I jumped back shaking. I heard fear-filled howling coming out of my mouth. "MOMMY!" I learned later that the strange animals were cars and trucks that were driving on a road.

Soon, a blue car stopped. A person got out of it and started walking towards me. Mr.

Farmer was a person and he was nice. I wondered if this person was nice and could take me back to my barn. As the person came closer, I lay down and cried. I was scared and too tired to run.

The person reached out her hand to me. "It is okay, girl. Are you hungry?" She had something that smelled like food. They were tasty orange colored crackers. How did she know I was hungry? I ate them quickly and sniffed for more.
The person said, "I'm Kara. Don't be afraid."
She gave me water from a cup. I was so thirsty. I started to like this person.

Kara picked me up and carried me to her blue car. "Get in my car, puppy," she said. "You are safe with me. I am so happy you didn't get hit by the other cars." She had a little person inside. Her name was Haley. Her high-pitched voice made my ears hurt. She kept screaming, "Hi Doggie!"
"Don't be so loud, Haley. She is scared." said her person-mommy.

Kara drove around and stopped at houses where people lived. She asked them if

they had lost a dog. No one knew me. She looked for other dogs like me, hoping they would be my family. She couldn't find any. I wish I could talk like people. I would have told her about my barn and the giant tree. "Please find my barn." I thought.

She took me to her home. This is how a lot of animals find foster and adoptive homes. I hope Kara knows how to take care of puppies until they can go home.

For Children:

It's different for children who need help. Many children who can't stay home go to a place called the Department of Social Services. The Social Workers find grandparents, aunts, or uncles to care for the children. If they can't find any family members to care for the children, there are special foster families who know how to take care of the children while their parents are being helped. They do not want children to be scared. Foster parents know children miss their families. They want to help them go back home.

On your life book pages, write your story of what you remember about why you came to stay in a foster home. Add these to your Life Book.

Pages 107 & 109

COMING INTO FOSTER CARE

I remember some things about the day I came to live in foster care. It really helps to know what happened. I used to think I did something bad that caused me not to go back home to my doggie birth family. My person foster mom, Kara, said that I wasn't a bad puppy. My doggie birth mom and dad just had problems taking care of me. Parents can love you and still have trouble taking care of their puppies.

For Children:

It is the same way with people, too. Sometimes, mommies and daddies can't take care of their children. They can love their children a lot. Parents need to be able to give children food to eat and a safe place to live. It is not the children's fault when families have problems. Children and parents may need people outside of their birth family to help them.

• Ask your social worker, your birth parents, foster parents or your adopted parents why you came to live in a foster home.

• Ask if there are people helping your parents.

• Are your birth parents using the help offered to them? If not, ask why?

• If they are letting people help them, ask what are they doing.

MY FIRST DAY IN MY FOSTER HOME

When Kara carried me from the road, she kept rubbing my head and saying, "Everything is going to be okay."

I was stinky and dirty with matted fur. I had a sad face. Dogs don't cry a lot of tears but we do whimper. I was whimpering and shaking. I was hungry and my stomach felt sick. I was scared.

I remember sitting in the back seat of the car. Kara didn't know that my name was Goldie Girl so she started calling me "Shelby." I liked that name but I wish she knew my real name. When we drove up into her driveway, I was very nervous and my stomach was sick. I jumped out to use the bathroom in her front yard. Dogs can do that.

Then, Haley, Kara's three year old little girl, patted me on my back and said, "Let's go into my house, Shelby."

I thought about running away but I didn't know where to go. I decided to walk with her. I was scared and hung my head down. It was hard for me to go into the strange house. I stepped in and then backed out of the front door. It didn't look or smell like the hay in my barn. I longed for my hay bed and the berry smell of my mommy's fur. She always liked to eat the berries from the bush outside my barn. Kara saw I was afraid and tried to make me feel safe. She rubbed me behind my ears until I stopped shaking.

"Shelby, we are nice here. We won't hurt you. I want you to be happy."

I did not want to be hugged because I was not used to people hugging me. But scratching me behind my ears helped my stomach feel better. Kara told Haley my stomach was hurting because I was hungry and nervous.

For Children:

- *How did you feel when you saw the house you were going to stay in?*

- *What did it feel like when you first met the people and their pets?*

- *What are their names and ages?*

- *What pets do they have? What are their names?*

- *What other questions do you have about them?*

Page 111

MEETING BEAR

After I stepped into my foster family's house, I smelled something I liked. It wasn't my barn but I smelled another dog. Sniff. I was right. From around the corner, a big, long-haired, brown and black dog walked up to me. He was bigger than me. His tail was wagging to let me know he was friendly. His name was Bear. Bear did not look like me, but it was a relief to see another dog in the house. We sniffed each other. That is how dogs say "Hello." I thought the people were nice but I felt better with Bear showing me around the house and the backyard. He understood what dogs liked and he talked like me.

BEAR ANSWERS MY QUESTIONS

Bear asked me if I had any questions about living at Kara and Haley's house. I had plenty of questions.

- What rooms am I allowed into?
- Where do I sleep?
- Is anyone sleeping in the room with me?
- Where do I go to the bathroom?
- How do I let the people know I have to go to the bathroom?
- Can I go to the bathroom alone?
- What do I do if I am scared?

- Can I bark or whimper?
- Will I get food here?
- What food will I eat here?
- Where do I eat?
- Can we play here?
- Will I have my own toys?
- Can I play on the porch, in the front yard and in the back yard?
- Are there any more animals living here? Are they nice?
- Are the people nice all of the time?
- Will they play with me?
- How do I know when they like me?
- How do I know when they are mad at me?
- What do they do when they are mad?
- Do they hit their pets?
- Do they let their pets sit on their laps?

Bear laughed, "You have lots of questions, puppy! You're going to have fun here. We can play in the family room, the back porch and back yard. We don't play in Haley's bedroom because she is little and we are big. We might knock her over." Haley liked to play with us. I remember she rode on our backs like we were horses. She laughed when Bear sat down and she slid off his back.

Children like other children showing them around their house.

- *What do you remember about the first day you went to stay with your new foster family?*
- *Who made you feel safe?*
- *Who showed you around the house?*
- *Where do or did you sleep?*
- *Could you eat anytime or were there meal times?*
- *Could you get up and use the bathroom at night?*
- *Are the people nice?*
- *Did the dog growl at you or did he lick your face?*
- *What other questions did you have? If you are new to your foster home, what questions would you like to have answered?*

Pages 113 & 115

WHERE DO I SLEEP?

Bear showed me his old comfortable orange and green striped blanket. I wondered if we were going to share it. Then, Kara laid a soft red blanket on the floor. She folded it to make a bed.

She spoke softly, "Here girl, this is your own bed."

I never had my own blanket. I jumped on it and wiggled around. AHHHH---my very own bed. I wished I had some hay under the blanket.

Bear laughed, "Now if you want to, you can push your blanket up close to me." I enjoyed cuddling next to him because I was used to five puppies sleeping with me. I missed my brother and sisters. I was scared at night in the new house. I would jump every time the furnace turned on. VAROOM! Haley looked sad watching me jump up when the furnace noise scared me.

She gave me one of her big stuffed bears, "Here new doggie. My stuffed animals help me sleep. This can help you sleep."

When she gave me my own soft toy, it helped me to like Haley. I had an old brown shoe at my barn and it helped me sleep. I missed my old brown shoe. The new stuffed bear helped me sleep, too. Maybe one day, they will find my old brown shoe.

For Children:

- *What helps you to go to sleep?*
- *When you sleep, do you like to sleep with a favorite toy, pillow or blanket?*
- *Did you bring anything from your home?*
- *What do you miss from your old home?*
- *Do you like to have a light on when you go to bed?*
- *Do you like a fan running or a radio on?*
- *What sounds make you scared?*
- *What sounds make you feel safe?*
- *Do you like to sleep alone in the room or with someone else?*

Page 123

<u>WHERE AND WHAT DO I EAT?</u>

Bear led me into the kitchen and showed me a big bowl of water on the floor. "We dogs and cat drink from this bowl." Cat? No one mentioned cats. We will talk about that later. Then, Bear showed me his food bowl, "Don't eat out of my bowl unless I let you!" He growled to make sure I understood him. Kara heard Bear growl and ran into the kitchen.

"Here's your bowl, Shelby. You will eat your food every night from this bowl. I will give you treats during the day." Treats? I had never had treats before. Did they taste like berries? She gave me a doggie treat to taste and it was delicious. I liked getting treats.

I saw a bag of dog food. Is that all we have to eat? When it is gone, we might not have any more food. My mommy worried when Mr. Farmer stopped feeding us. We had to share the little bit of food we found. This is a new house and I didn't know how they feed their puppies. I tried to tear the bag open to eat up the food. Who knows if this is the last bag of dog food?

Kara pulled me back and yelled, "NO, SHELBY!"
She scared me and I laid down waiting to be hit. She didn't hit me.
She started rubbing my head, "Sorry, girl. I just wanted to stop you from tearing open the bag. I will feed you every day. Don't worry about food."

I did not believe her. She gave Bear and me some dog food to prove she was going to feed us. It was before supper time but she thought it would help me not to be scared. I was very hungry. I had been lost from my barn when Kara found me in the street. Eating dog food here tasted like steak to me. I was starting to like this place more and more. Still, it would take more days of eating here for me to believe we had enough food. Sometimes I would take a few pieces of my dog food and hide them under my red doggie blanket to make sure I would never be hungry again.

For Children:

- *When you first came to live with your foster family, did you know you would eat every day?*
- *What did your foster parents do to help you know you would have plenty of food in their home?*
- *What did your foster family do to help you know when the meals were served?*
- *What are your favorite foods?*
- *What are foods you do not like?*
- *What rooms do you eat in at your birth family's home?*
- *What rooms do you eat in at your foster home?*
- *Do you have a special place to sit?*
- *What are your favorite snacks?*
- *What snacks do you not like?*
- *Do you know how to make your own meals?*
- *What can you make?*

Page 125

WHERE AND WHEN CAN I USE THE BATHROOM?

I never lived in a house. I lived in a barn and we could use the bathroom anywhere in the barn or outside.

Bear told me, "You can't go to the bathroom in the house. You have to go outside. Just go to the back door and bark. Kara or Haley will open the door."

That was hard to remember. Kara let us go outside to potty before we went to bed. That helped me. There were times I had some accidents and went to the bathroom on the floor in the house but Kara did not act mad.

She petted my head and said, "I know you are confused and sad, Shelby. It's okay if you forget and wet on the floor. In time, you will learn to go outside." She was right. I did learn as I began to feel safer there.

She would give me a pat on the head and say, "Good girl."

For Children:

- *How did you find the bathroom?*
- *What did you do to feel safe using the new bathroom?*
- *Can you use the bathroom at night? Are there rules?*
- *Do you like to have a light on so you can find the bathroom at night?*
- *How did you learn to turn the sink faucet off and on?*
- *How did you learn to turn the bathtub and shower knobs off and on?*
- *Did you know it was okay to have accidents?*

BEAR'S AND MY FAVORITE PLACE

The screened-in porch at the back of the house was Bear's favorite place to lie down. He liked to look out into the back yard and watch the birds and the squirrels. The back yard was where we would run and play. I didn't like to lie down and watch the squirrels.

I would say, "Come on Bear, let's chase the squirrels!"
"Naw, I am happy just lying here in the sun," Bear would say.

Bear told me that Kara and her friends liked to sit out in the back yard and play with us. Kara and her friends threw balls so we could chase them. Chase was my favorite game. I started having fun! My tail was wagging a lot. I was a little confused. I missed my home, family and friends but I was happy here too. Kara told me I could love both families.

Bear taught me how to get the people to rub us.
He gave me pointers. "Now, walk over to a person and lay your head in their lap and look up at them with sad eyes."
People loved it. It worked! I got rubbed a lot, especially behind my ears!

I think the backyard was my favorite place. There was a huge tree with long branches. I would lay under them when it was hot outside. The shade was cool. It felt a little like the giant tree next to my barn. I always fell asleep under the tree and dreamed about being home.

- *What does your foster family like to do at their house or in their yard?*
- *Where are your favorite places in the house and yard?*
- *Why are they your favorite places?*
- *How do you like to have fun with the family?*
- *What are your favorite games to play?*
- *Share with your foster family your favorite places and games?*
- *If you are not in your foster home now, what do you remember about living there?*

Pages 119 & 121

MEETING SASSY THE CAT

It took some time to understand how these people lived. They had lots of rooms, a big box with cold food inside it called a refrigerator, and a cat.

Let's talk about the cat. When I arrived at Kara and Haley's house, I looked around for other animals. Living in my barn, we had lots of animals walking around and sleeping near us. I had a cat friend named "Cat." She was fluffy, yellow and white. I was a puppy and she was a kitten. We would play with sticks and jump over rocks together. We would laugh and run. She was my best friend. We didn't care that she was a cat and I was a dog. I missed her when the people at the barn took all of the animals away.

So when I saw a cat in this house I was excited. But the cat in this house hid from me. One day, she yelled "MEOW" as she jumped on me and scratched my leg. Ouch! Her different shades of gray fur stood up on her back. She scared me. She was older and the biggest cat I had ever seen. When she hissed at me, one long fang tooth hung from the top of her mouth. I didn't do anything to her. I never barked, growled or chased her.

Then she told me, "I don't want you here. We already have one dog."

She hurt my feelings.

I whined back at her, "I did not ask to come live here either. But if I can't live with my mommy, I want to stay here."

And I wanted everyone to like me, even Sassy.

I told Bear what happened. He talked to me and made me feel better.

He explained, "Sassy was Haley's first animal. She was born here and has lived all of her life in this house. Sassy wants Haley to love her forever and is afraid other animals will take her place. When I first came to live with them, Kara and Haley played a lot with me. This worried her."

Sassy didn't like to play rough like Bear. She would lie on the back of the couch and look outside at her laughing people playing games with Bear. She would meow a sad meow. Haley and Kara would come into the house. They would pick up Sassy and hold her. They didn't understand "animal talk" but they tried to make her happy.

I felt sorry for Sassy and I gave her a wet lick to let her know I was not going to take her place. It took a long time but Sassy started liking me.

I told her, "No other animal would ever take your people's love from you."

I could tell she started liking me because she stopped scratching me. She hissed at me but never scratched me again. Her hissing became a game with us. Her one fang stopped scaring me and I liked hearing her tell stories of when she was young like me.

Page 129

For Children:

Like animals, children sometimes have trouble getting adults to understand them.

- **When you moved into a new house, did you feel another child did not want you there?**
- **What were the reasons why the child did not like you?**
- **How did someone explain to you that it wasn't your fault that other children were sad or mad?**
- **Why would the other children in the house feel jealous, sad or mad?**
- **Have you tried to tell adults something but you couldn't get them to understand? The foster parents' children may have the same problem.**
- **How did that make you feel?**
- **What are ways that you use to get the adults attention?**

Sometimes children are tired of sharing their toys, pets and parents. Sometimes they feel the new child will be liked more than them. This usually goes away after the children in the house start playing and having fun together. Parents can talk to all of the children and tell them how everyone is special. Parents can love many children at the same time. It's helpful for all of the children to talk about how they feel. It's okay to ask for time alone with the parents. If everyone feels important, they can start being friends with each other.

MISSING MY BIRTH FAMILY

I felt confused when I came to Kara and Haley's house. I had plenty of food to eat and a soft red blanket to sleep on. The people were friendly and Bear became my friend. But every day I missed my doggie family and my barn. My mom couldn't find enough food for us but that didn't mean she did not love us. I missed her. As long as I could snuggle beside her I was happy. My daddy left us to find food when I was a little puppy and I still missed him. My brother and sisters loved his powerful voice and playful ways.

I am afraid I will forget my life with my birth doggie-family. I don't want to forget that Mr. Farmer called my mommy Sadie. He called my daddy Duke. I called them Mommy and Daddy. I am scared I will forget how their barks sound and how they smelled like blueberries. I don't want to forget the stories they told us, like when we were born.

Mommy said, "I was so excited about having puppies. I made a soft bed out of hay. When it was time for you to be born I lay down until all six of you were born safely. You were the fourth puppy and your daddy and I named you Goldie Girl. That was your grandmother's name and you look like her."

I have two older sisters, one older brother and two younger sisters. Daddy said we are proud Golden Retriever dogs. My fur is soft and dark golden like my mommy's fur. My large golden brown eyes look like my daddy's eyes. My brother, sisters and I look alike but we are different. Some of us are dark golden and others are light golden. Some are bigger than others.

Being a family of Golden Retrievers is special and fun. We all belong together.

I remember playing with my brother and sisters. We wrestled and played hide and seek. We would fall down and roll on our backs and laugh. If we hurt each other, we would make up with licks and touching each other's noses. Those memories make me feel good inside and sad because I miss them.

My birth doggie-family had problems but it did not matter to me. They are my family and I miss them. I wish my doggie family could live here with me at Kara's house. There is plenty of food here.

I had questions. Was I going to live with Kara and Haley forever? On the third day, Kara saw me looking out through the backyard fence. I had been sitting there for hours. My tail didn't wag because I was sad missing my family. She sat down beside me and patted my head. "Shelby, I am looking for your doggie family. When I find them, I will try and help bring you all back together." She explained I would stay with her family for as long as I needed.

She told me, "I will tell you everything I know about your life. I want you to feel comfortable with us. It is okay for you to dream and talk about your family. I wish I knew doggie-talk so I could listen to your family stories."

She was going to try and find pictures of Golden Retrievers to help me feel closer to my family. She didn't know what it was like being a Golden Retriever but she would try to find out what I needed. She would buy a doggie brush for my long golden fur. She would ask an animal doctor what I needed to remain healthy. Kara made me feel better being there. She made me feel important.

I wish Kara did understand doggie-talk. I have a special doggie-family. I miss my mommy nuzzling me with her nose and cuddling with me. I miss my brother and sisters playing with me. I wondered if they knew where I was and did they miss me? If I was a person, I could tell Kara my family stories. She could help me write them in a special book called a Life Book so that I could look at it when

I needed to remember. I would be able to feel special being a Golden Retriever with sad memories and a ton of happy memories. I like thinking about the happy memories.

For Children:

Children stay in foster homes until their parents can become strong enough to care for their children. This could take a few months or several years. Every family needs different kinds of help.

Children can talk to their foster parents about their birth families and keep photos of them. There are special things about their birth families to make them feel proud and loved. Maybe their birth mom sang a certain song to them or their birth dad made them laugh. It can make children feel closer to their foster parents if they can talk about their birth family. Writing these stories down will help children to remember their birth family.

Share your birth family stories and photos with your foster family. Frame your family photos or add them to your life book.

Pages 143— 159

VISITS WITH BIRTH PARENTS

If Kara could find my birth doggie mother and father, maybe my mommy would bring me my favorite old brown shoe. I slept with that old shoe, chewed on it and played with it. Maybe they would bring me some hay to sleep on until I can go home. I could cuddle with them. I could play with my brother and sisters. I would love for my mommy and daddy to be friends with Haley, Kara, Sassy and Bear. We could all be close forever. I hope my doggie family is happy. Maybe a new person family is feeding my birth family and soon I will go home with them.

For Children:

Most birth parents do visit their children. Foster parents want the visits to be meaningful for all of the birth family members. Foster parents try to sit down and talk with the children's birth parents. The birth parents and foster parents share stories about the children such as what the children like and dislike. They make plans on how they are going to take care of the children together. It's called Shared Parenting. Children like it when their foster parents and birth parents get along.

Social workers help children visit with their parents. At visits there are games to play, books to read, coloring books and "Life Books" to work on. Visits can be fun and sad. At each visit children need to know when they will see their birth family again. A calendar could help children count down the days. Even though saying goodbye is difficult, it is important to see their family.

Some birth parents have a lot of problems and cannot visit their children. Sometimes birth parents aren't healthy and they may need special people to help them get well. There are many people who try and help parents. There are judges, guardian ad litems, social workers, therapists and teachers who work with parents.

Questions you may have about visiting your parents:

- When can I visit with my parents?
- Will my brothers and sisters be there?
- When can I visit my grandparents, aunts, uncles and cousins?
- Will I ever be able to see my old friends again?
- Where are the visits? Can I have the visits in a fun place?
- Can I bring a picture I drew or photo to give to my family?
- Can I bring a picnic or snacks to share with my family?
- Can they bring me some of my favorite things from home?
- Can we take pictures of our family together at our visit?

CAN I SHOW MY REAL FEELINGS?

People laughed here. Bear laughed. I guessed it was okay for me to laugh, too. Of course, it's hard to see smiles on a dog's face. You have to look at their tails. Bear and I wagged our tails when we were happy. I was shocked to see my tail wagging. I must have been feeling some happy feelings. It's okay to feel mixed feelings.

Sometimes, I was scared or confused. Sometimes, I was excited and happy.

Kara was so good at understanding my mixed feelings. She would say, "Are you sad, Shelby? Do you want me to pet you?"

Sometimes I would want her to pet me but there were times I wanted to lay on my blanket alone. She never was mad at me. Haley wanted me to be happy all of the time but Kara explained I missed my family and my home. When Kara had blueberries in the kitchen, I felt sad, happy and mad. Blueberries reminded me of my mommy and I missed her.

Haley thought her house with all of the tasty food was better than what my doggie-mommy would give me. Haley wondered why I wasn't happy here. Kara told her my family and home had happy and sad memories. She said all my family memories were for me to keep. I missed the smells, the sounds, playing with my brother and sisters. Especially, I missed my mommy licking my face. That is how dogs say, "I love you" or "You need to wash your face."

Feelings are okay. We cannot control our emotions. We can control what we do with them.

HAPPY

How do you show you are happy?

- Do you laugh out loud?
- Do you giggle?
- Do you have a big smile on your face?
- Do you jump up and down?

SAD

When I am whimpering I am telling everyone I am scared or need help. I am sad when I think about my family. I wonder where they are and if they are okay. I am sad because I know they miss me. I was sad when I was lost from my family. I was sad the first night I stayed in my foster home. I did not know anyone or any of the animals there. I was sad because the bed and food were different. I was sad because I missed my old brown shoe. Bear said this is all right to do. Children cry when they are sad. I cannot cry tears so I whimper. I whimper when I feel lonely or miss my family. I whimper when I don't remember the rules. I whimper when I am depressed or sad. I wish dogs could use words.

Bear tried to help me to stop being sad. He would lie beside me and licked my face. He could not stop my sadness but he did make me feel better. He became my best friend.

For Children:

Children can use words to tell people how they are feeling. Then, people can help them feel better. Children feel sad when they leave their families. They are sad when they move into a stranger's home. They are sad when they miss their toys and pillows. It helps when their foster parents help them understand why they are sad. Children who live with them in their foster homes can help them not to feel alone. Adults can help them visit their birth families. When children see their foster family trying to help them they can start caring for them. There will be sad times but they won't feel alone.

How do you show you are sad?

- *Do you cry?*
- *Do you crawl up in a ball on the bed?*
- *Do you tell someone you are sad?*
- *Do you want to be alone?*
- *Do you want someone to hold you?*

All of these ways are okay.

ANGRY

Bear growled at me when I was near his bowl. So I thought growling was okay to do any time.

Bear warned me, "Don't ever growl at Haley or Kara. It is okay to growl if someone is mean to them or is trying to break into our house. You can growl at the squirrels outside."

When people came over to the house, Kara would tell me if I could growl at them. When dogs growl, they want you to stay back and not come near them. When dogs growl at other dogs they are saying to stay away from their things or their food. They may growl if they think you are going to hurt them or hurt the ones they love. Bear said Kara would tell me to "Hush" if I growled at the wrong time.

For Children:

Children can be angry at other children who take their toys. They can be angry at having to do homework or chores. They can be angry that they are not living at home with their birth family. They can be angry because it is difficult living with people they don't know well. They can be angry at their parents for letting them go to a foster home. They can be angry at themselves for not being able to fix their family. Sometimes, there are the little things that happen that release the anger inside of children and adults. Things like someone using their stuff or having to get up early for school. Sometimes they don't know why they are angry.

How do you show you are mad or angry?

- *Do you yell?*
- *Do you throw things?*
- *Do you break things?*
- *Do you run?*
- *Do you tell someone you are mad?*
- *Do you want to be left alone?*
- *Do you hit things?*
- *Do you hit people or animals?*
- *Do you cry?*

It's okay to be angry. Try not to act in ways that are against the rules. Most rules say do not hurt a person or animals. Sometimes, breaking things might be against the rules. What kinds of things might you throw or hit safely? Things like throwing a basketball in the net or hitting a pillow. Ask your birth parents, foster parents, or social workers what are ways are okay to show anger.

HOW DO OTHER PEOPLE SHOW THEIR ANGER?

Bear said Kara does not yell a lot but when she needed you to immediately stop what you were doing, she may yell. She did not hit you but she might make you stay in the backyard if you make a mess inside the house. She would yell at you if you made Haley cry. Kara tried to keep little Haley from being hurt. I remember my mommy growling at raccoons if they came too close to her puppies. My mommy would growl and show her teeth. She tried to keep us all safe.

She would growl if my brother, sisters and I played too rough. I realized that even if Kara yelled at you, she still liked you.

For Children:

Ask your foster parents how you will know when they are angry.

- *How do the other family members show anger?*
- *What makes them angry?*
- *What do they want you to do if they are angry?*
- *Will they still like you if they are angry at you?*

Share how your birth parents showed their feelings. This is important to talk about because you may have lived with different families and it can be confusing for you. You have learned many ways to handle feelings from all of the people who have raised you.

Pages: Foster Care: 131 — 141, Adoption: 197 — 209

JUMPING JACK GOES HOME : REUNIFICATION

I knew my mommy was still looking for me. Kara kept searching for my mommy. But with animals, it can be difficult to find their families after being separated.

A new friend joined our foster family. Jumping Jack had hurt his leg and Kara found him on our front porch steps. Rabbits can't survive if they can't hop around. Kara felt sorry for my new friend and took him to the animal doctor called a veterinarian. The doctor bandaged Jumping Jack's leg.

The doctor told Kara, "It will be a month before you can set this little guy free to find his rabbit family."

Jumping Jack and I talked a lot about our rabbit and doggie birth families. We missed them deeply. He had a mommy, a daddy, a grandmother, and eight brothers and sisters. His family lived under an old green shed near our house. He wanted to tell Kara where he lived but people don't understand "rabbit talk." I asked him how he hurt himself.

"I was out hopping around when I caught

"

my leg on a toy wagon in your front yard and twisted it. I was hurting and couldn't hop so I dragged myself to your porch steps. I was lucky that Kara is a kind person. I can't wait to hop again."

Jumping Jack kept trying to hop on his hurt leg. That is how he got his name from Kara.

She said, "You are one jumping jack rabbit. I am going to call you Jumping Jack."

Jumping Jack's family came to the back fence every day to visit him. They missed him and he missed them.

"We will take you home when you are better," they would say.
He introduced me to his birth family as his friend. Kara saw his family at the fence and she would take carrots out for all the rabbits to eat.

Jumping Jack and I played in the backyard. I had to be careful not to step on him. Days and days went by. Then one day, his leg stopped hurting and it became stronger. Kara took off his bandage. He hopped all over the house and the backyard. Kara told Jumping Jack that she would help him go home.

She didn't know rabbit or dog talk so we couldn't tell her Jumping Jack's family was already waiting for him at the backyard fence. I was so excited for Jumping Jack.

"You can go home! I will help you."

So I dug a hole under the fence and he crawled under it! Jumping Jack and his family were so happy. They all hopped up and down. I was happy for them but I also felt sad.

I called out to him, "Jumping Jack, what about me? I am your friend and I will miss you!"

He hopped over to the fence, "Don't worry. My family and I will come back to see you. Maybe one day, you can dig a bigger hole so you can crawl under the fence and play with us."

"Great idea! I love to run and play."

Kara, Haley, Bear and Sassy walked out the door just in time to see Jumping Jack and his family hopping across the front yard towards their home.

Kara smiled. "Good bye, Jumping Jack! Come back to see us!"

For Children:

Going home can be happy and sad. Children want to be with their family but they want to be safe and to be taken care of, given food, clothes, and the other things they need. Before going home, birth parents visit their children to let them know they love them. Parents can tell their children what they are doing to prepare for them to come home.

Children can show their birth parents their school work, art work and give their parents pictures of them. Children need to see their family so they can remember them. It would be great to have a camera to take pictures when on a visit. They can share the pictures with their birth parents. They can frame and hang their pictures in their rooms.

When the judge says it is okay to go home, foster parents help children pack their clothes, toys and other belongings. Children need to take their Life Books full of pictures, stories and memories. Children miss their foster family when they leave to go home. It helps make the leaving less hurtful if they know when they will see their foster family again.

Page 169

GROWING UP WITH ANOTHER FAMILY: ADOPTION

Living with Kara, Haley, Bear and Sassy felt comfortable and safe. Kara looked for my doggie family but we couldn't find them. I knew it was okay to be sad. I won't forget my doggie family, and maybe, I will see them again one day.

Bear and I grew bigger and bigger. We had fun playing "rough and tumble." Sometimes we would accidentally knock Haley down. When she cried, we always licked her to say we were sorry. I lived there for two years. As I grew bigger, the house and the yard seemed smaller to me. I liked to dig holes under the fence and climb under it and run all through the neighborhood. I would play with Jumping Jack and his family. I loved to run long distances. It reminded me of when I ran with my brother and sisters at my barn. Kara constantly had to find me in the neighborhood and bring me back home. She wasn't mad but she was worried.

She cried, "Shelby, you have to stop leaving the yard! I don't want you to get lost or hurt. Please stay in the yard!"

Kara's best friend, Shannon, told her, "Shelby needs more land to run on. You love her but you can't keep her in the yard. My parents live in country with lots of land to run on. You know how they love their pets. You could bring Haley and Bear out to play with Shelby anytime. Shelby could come out and visit you, Sassy, Bear and Haley."

Kara loved me and it was hard for her to think about me living somewhere else. I could tell she was sad because she kept petting me over and over again. Kara told me I might go live with another family. If I liked them and they liked me, I could adopt them as my new family. She told me that a dog, two goats and two horses lived there. I would have lots of land to run on and no one would tie me up or put me in a small fence. I liked that but I still did not want to leave my foster family.

Kara said, "You aren't bad and leaving here is not your fault. We want you to be happier."

Shannon asked her parents to come over to Kara's house to meet me. I was nervous and when I get nervous, I jump up on people and lick them. As soon as Donna and Tony came in the door I jumped up on them.

"Well, how are you, girl?" Donna giggled. She was not angry at me for jumping on her. Tony laughed at me. They both petted me and kept saying,"Shelby, you're beautiful!"

I liked playing with Donna and Tony. I rolled on my back and they rubbed my belly. That felt fantastic! I wanted to come visit them and hopefully get my belly rubbed again. I wanted to see the land with lots of room to run. Maybe my barn was out there.

Five days later, Kara, Haley and Shannon took Bear and me for a ride to see Donna and Tony's land. We had fun riding in the car. We enjoyed putting our heads out the windows to feel the wind blowing our ears up in the air.
I barked at Bear,"Look, the trees look like the trees at my barn!"

My stomach felt excited. Kara called all the trees and land the "country." When the car doors opened, we jumped out. Tony and Donna were standing in front of a white house with flowers all around it. I ran over to the flowers jumping up to catch butterflies. They were flying everywhere! I couldn't catch them. Bear and I ran around barking and laughing.

 Kara told me to "hush" but Tony said, "It's okay to bark out in the country." Wow! There is a lot of land out here to play on. Holding her arms up in the air, Haley ran around with us.

Kara took me inside to see the house. A small gray animal came prancing into the room.

I asked, "What is that? Oh, it's a dog! A really small dog."

I jumped over to it to say hello. I must have jumped too quickly because he barked at me to "watch out." I stepped back and waited for the dog to come to me. Donna told me his name was Toby and he was a Shih Tzu dog. That sounds fancy. All I knew, he was small and I better be careful not to step on him. Donna and Tony adopted Toby four years ago. He let me know that he did not want to leave Donna and Tony's house just because I was there. I remember how Sassy the cat felt. Donna picked up Toby and told him they could love both of us. We could all be one big happy family. She put Toby down and we sniffed each other. Toby calmed down and walked around with me. I was glad he didn't jump on me like Sassy did that first day at Kara's house.

I followed him around the house.

"I like your house, Toby. There are so many doors and windows to look outside. I can run from one end of the house to the other end. I like to run."

Toby just looked up at me. "You are one big dog!"

After playing for a few hours, Bear and I climbed back into the car. I gave Donna and Tony a lick before I left. I had so much fun. Kara and Donna talked for a few minutes before Kara got back into the car. On the way home, Kara talked to Haley about Donna and Tony adopting me.

Haley cried sad tears. "But I love Shelby," she said.

Bear and I talked to each other about my moving and then we were quiet. I think I heard Kara crying too. Sometimes, doing what is best can hurt.

We all had a special time that night. Haley hugged me over and over.

She brushed me. "I love you, Shelby. You can have all of my toys, if you want them. I don't want you to go."

Bear let me eat out of his bowl. Sassy lay next to me and purred. Haley gave me one of her favorite toys.

Kara hugged me, "I am so happy I found you, girl. You are so sweet and you make us laugh."

She shared that she gave Donna and Tony all the information about where she found me. That way, my adoptive family can help me find my birth family.

She talked about Donna and Tony being a nice family to grow up with. I could run all day long in the pastures. I watched Kara packing up my toys, leash, food and treats. She was sad because she didn't say a word as she put my things into a box. I guessed tomorrow was the day I would move. I held onto the promise that we would see each other again. I slept little on my red blanket that night. I was sad. I was going to miss the furnace sounds that scared me my first night here. I would miss the smells of fresh baked biscuits and cherry lotions. And I would miss my favorite tree with the long branches. But most of all, I would miss my Haley, Kara, Bear and Sassy.

Animals move into their adopted homes more quickly. Animals can't tell people how they feel and that it's hard to move.

For Children:

Foster parents fall in love with the children who live with them. In addition to loving the children who live with them, part of being a foster parent is helping children prepare to go home or to be adopted.

Social workers put a lot of work into helping birth parents bring their children back home with them. Some birth parents have a very difficult time. There are times when birth parents are not healthy enough to take care of their children. Sometimes social workers cannot find their birth parents. Children may grow up in another family. This is called an adoptive family. Adoptive parents want to love and take care of children that cannot go back home to their birth families. Children can have three families: their birth family, their foster family and their adoptive family. Some foster parents adopt the children they were fostering. Many adoptive parents continue to involve the children's birth family and foster family in their adoptive children's lives. Children can have a lot of families who love them and children can love all of their families. Children need to move slowly into adoptive homes. It's called "transition."

Children visit and spend more time with their adoptive families before they move into their home. How did you feel when you were told you were going to be adopted?

- *Who told you about being adopted?*
- *Could you talk about your feelings? Who did you talk to?*
- *How did you meet your adoptive family?*
- *Where were you when you met your adoptive family?*
- *What did they do or say to make you feel better?*
- *What did you want them to do?*
- *How long after you met them, did you move into your new home?*
- *What did you take with you to your adoptive home?*
- *How did you say goodbye to your foster family?*
- *What plans were made for you to see your foster family again?*

MOVING INTO MY ADOPTIVE HOME

Kara and Shannon made plans to take Bear and I to Donna and Tony's house. I knew I was adopting them today but I wasn't sure how I was going to feel. Haley stayed with her grandmother. Bear and I jumped into the back of Kara's car. We wrestled and then took our places looking out the windows to let the wind blow our ears up in the air. My stomach hurt as I watched Haley standing in the driveway waving goodbye to me. My tail stopped wagging. A sad feeling made me shake. Kara drove to pick Shannon up before we went to the country.

Shannon kept talking to Kara, "Shelby is going to love living with my parents. You can always come out and see her." Kara had those tears coming out of her eyes again.

When we drove up to the white house, Donna and Tony walked out to greet us. I guess I was happy and nervous. I jumped up on them again. They laughed and said, "Down, girl. Go chase butterflies!" I called out to Bear to come and run with me. We ran and ran.

Bear and I were pulling each other's tails when Kara called Bear's name. We ran back to her. She opened the back hatch of the car which was our signal to hop in.

Bear ran and jumped in but when I tried, Kara grabbed my collar and pulled me back, saying, "Shelby, you stay here. We will be back next weekend."

Bear touched his nose to mine and Kara hugged me. I liked her hugs, now.

Shannon rubbed my head, said "goodbye," and they all drove away. I tried to run after the car but Donna and Tony held me.

"It's okay, girl," they said.

Those were the same words Kara said when she picked me up off the street two years earlier. She made me happy. Maybe, Donna and Tony will make everything okay, too. It's hard starting all over again.

MY FIRST DAY IN MY ADOPTIVE HOME

Tony and Donna led me into their house. My head hung low and my tail did not wag. I was so sad. I didn't want to get to know another family. It is so hard.

Toby ran up to me and started sniffing me. "You will like it here. They are a kind people family," he said.

I was glad he was already my friend. It made it easier for me to stay. I followed him to where the family watches TV.

Donna put a huge dog pillow down on the floor.
"Shelby, here is a big tan and green pillow just right for a beautiful Golden Retriever. It is your new bed."

Toby's dog bed was little. I looked at Toby's bed and wondered if it was as comfortable as my new bed.

Toby shook his head, "You silly dog! You can't fit in my bed."

"I still want to try and lay down in it," I responded.

I put my paws in the bed and turned around and around until I thought I could squeeze into the bed. I tried it and every time half my body would fall out onto the floor. Everyone laughed watching me try to fit into Toby's bed. My tail wagged. I liked my soft pillow more when Donna laid my red blanket on it. It smelled like Kara and Haley's house with cherry lotion. I could smell Bear and Sassy when I laid on it. It made me feel closer to my foster family.

As I lay on my bed, I remembered moving in with Kara and Haley. I never lived in a house before Kara's house so getting used to it was tricky. Hopefully, this move would be easier now that I had learned more about living in houses. Like my other house, when I stood at the door and barked, Tony and Donna let me out to use the bathroom or to play. They gave me my own food bowl. I noticed there was plenty of dog food so I wasn't worried about having enough to eat. I didn't need to hide food under my pillow. Toby and I drank water out of the same bowl. Donna gave me my toys from Kara's house and a new dog collar. What excited me the most was that Donna gave me an "old black shoe." An old shoe! How did she know that I missed my old brown shoe? It wasn't my old brown shoe but the black shoe smelled and tasted like my old brown shoe.

That first night, both dog beds were next to each other in Donna and Tony's bedroom. I tucked my new black shoe and the stuffed bear Haley gave to me under my red blanket. There was a humming sound and Toby told me it was a fan. I liked that sound.

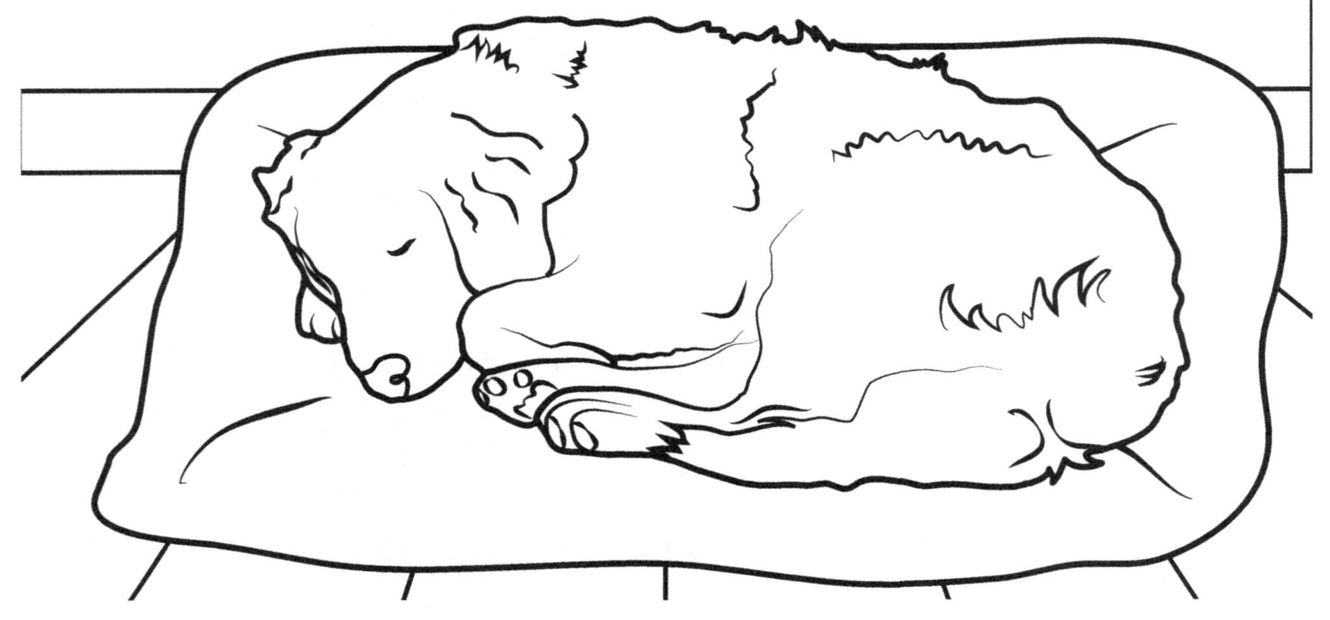

Everyone settled into their beds and Donna petted our heads and said, "Good night, sweethearts."

I felt safe. I woke up a few times during the night thinking I was at my old house. I whimpered a sad and lost feeling. Donna moved my bed next to her bed where she could rub my head until I fell asleep. I then slept peacefully with my stuffed bear and my new black shoe.

- *Do you remember the first day you moved in your adoptive home?*
- *What were some of your feelings that first day?*
- *Was it easier moving in because you knew the family?*
- *Who helped you learn about living in your adoptive home?*
- *What things were the same?*
- *What new things did you have to learn?*
- *Who did you feel close to that first day? Why?*
- *How did you feel that first night?*
- *Where do you sleep?*
- *Do you sleep in your own bedroom or do you share a room?*
- *What sounds did you not like?*
- *What sounds did you like?*
- *What helped you to feel more comfortable?*
- *What did you bring with you to help you sleep?*
- *Did you sleep all night or did you wake up during that night?*
- *How long did it take for you to start sleeping all night?*
- *Who helped you feel comfortable and safe at night?*
- *What did they do?*
- *Now, what makes you happy in your adoptive home?*

Page 173-183

TOBY'S STORY: PHYSICAL ABUSE

Toby had trouble trusting me. He would be nice to me and then all of a sudden, he would bark at me. I made sure I didn't step on him and I let him drink out of the water bowl with me. I told him he could sleep next to me anytime he wanted to. I never growled at him. Still, he would push me away. I was confused.

One day after he nipped at me, I asked him what I did to make him not like me. He looked startled and said, "I like you, Shelby. I just have to be careful. Animals and people can hurt me."

I was surprised at his answer and I asked, "Toby, has any person or animal hurt you here? Everyone seems so nice and they care for us."

He shook his head as he answered, "No one has hurt me here but I have been hurt before and I am afraid it might happen again."
I asked Toby who hurt him and when did it happen.

We lay down on the floor and he told me his story.

"When I was born, I was the smallest puppy in a litter of seven puppies. My mommy didn't like the smallest puppies because they were weak.

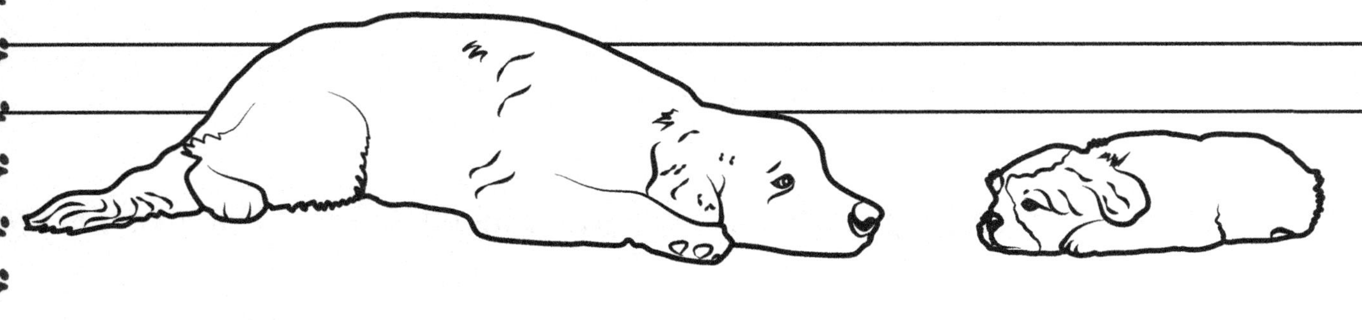

"She would let the five biggest puppies eat first. The smallest puppy next to me was my sister. We ate what was left over after the other puppies had eaten. It was hard to wait. When we tried to eat with the others, Mommy would bite at us and make us wait. Mommy wasn't treated well by her people owner. The man would kick her and made us stay outside in the rain and cold. He didn't feed her every day so she was hungry. She tried to take care of us but it was too hard. Our daddy left us, so mommy was alone with seven puppies. When she was hungry and cold she would be mean to us. I loved my mommy even though she would bite or leave us out in the rain.

"One day, people started coming to see us. One after one, my brothers and sisters were taken to live at other people's houses. I wanted to go with them because they might have food and a warm place to sleep. Finally, a kind person came to see me. I knew she was kind because she gently picked me up and kissed the top of my head.

"She asked the owner, 'Why hasn't anyone picked this sweet little puppy to take home?'

"The mean man said, 'No one wants a puny runt.'

"She looked at him and replied, 'I want him. He is adorable and I will love him.'

"She took me home and gave me a bath. She fed me out of my own bowl and gave me my own bed. Being a small gray and white Shih Tzu was fun because I went everywhere with my person. I heard people call her Memaw so that is what I called her.

"I remember she told me, 'You are a strong dog because you survived many weeks without food and shelter. I am going to name you Toby, which is a strong name.'

"Memaw made my life happier. Still, I missed my birth family. I wondered if the mean man was hurting my mommy. I wished I could give her some of my food. I bet she wouldn't bite me anymore. I missed my mommy, my sisters, and my brothers. If a nice person could pick my mommy up and take her to their house, she would be happy. Maybe we could all see each other again. I worried about my mommy and that caused me to have accidents in the house. Memaw understood why I would go to the bathroom on the floors. I tried to wait to go outside.

"She said, 'Puppies that are worried or hurt by others sometimes have accidents.' She couldn't let me outside alone because I would run away. I didn't want to run away. I guess I wanted to find my mommy. Memaw wasn't mad at me. She kept me close to her and let me know she loved me.

"After a few months, Memaw's house became the home I was going to grow up in. She adopted me and we were so happy being a family. Memaw got sick one day and I saw people trying to help her. I was upset and started wetting on the floors again. I licked her to let her know I was close by and would take care of her.

"As time went on, it was harder for Memaw to move around. Her daughter, Donna, told people Memaw had cancer. Donna and Tony took care of her. Donna and Tony drove her to the doctor a lot and stayed with her all of the time. Donna would hold me and pet me like Memaw did. Two years later, Memaw was in her bed and I lay on her lap. I knew something was wrong with her. She then stopped breathing and went to heaven. I whimpered and whimpered. Donna and Tony told me I had made Memaw very happy! I couldn't believe I lost someone else that I loved. I wondered if everyone I loved would leave me.

"Donna and Tony took me to their house. It was beside my Memaw's house and I played there a lot so I was comfortable. They told me I was going to be adopted by them. I wondered if I did something to make my birth doggie-mommy angry and my Memaw go to heaven. Donna told me, 'You don't cause adults to do anything. Adults take care of children and puppies.'

"Donna helped me feel better even though I was sad. I liked to go over to my old house and smell my Memaw. I liked to listen to my people talking about their memories of Memaw. I was in a lot of those memories which made me feel closer to her. After weeks with Donna and Tony holding me and taking care of me, I started calling them Momma Donna and Papa Tony. I want to trust you, Shelby. When I feel close to you, it scares me. I don't want you to leave me, too. Give me time to be your brother."

I was patient and as time went by, Toby started playing with me. We ran up and down the fence line together and talked about our lives. We had a lot in common. We love our birth families and the other families who love us. He even started sleeping beside me. I think he felt safe next to me.

For Children:

Sometimes, children come into foster care because they were physically abused by one or both parents. Abuse means someone hurt them. Children are confused about why their parents would hurt them. Parents can be out of control and hurt the children they love. Children don't cause their parents to hit, grab or do other things that hurt. Parents could be sick, worried, taking drugs or living with an adult who hurts people. There are also parents who don't hurt their children but don't stop others from hurting them. We don't know all of the reasons that cause parents to lose their tempers. It is never the children's fault when adults hurt them. Children should never be hurt. When it happens, children go stay with other family members or to a foster family so they can be safe and not be hurt. Sometimes children can move to several homes before growing up in one home. There are people to help their parents and work to help their families live together again. Sometimes, parents can't live with their children because they have trouble taking care of their children. Children can always love their parents even if they can't go home. Foster parents and adoptive parents understand that it is hard for children to trust them. It takes time for children to believe other adults will not hurt them. Children should never be hurt by anyone.

- Were you hurt at home?
- Did you ask anyone to help you or were your afraid to tell anyone?
- Who did you tell?
- Did you know your parents can love you and still hurt you?
- Did someone tell you why your parent hurt you?
- You can ask your social worker, therapist or foster parent

to help you understand why your parent hurt you.

- Did anyone tell you that your parent's anger is not your fault?

- You can talk to your foster parent, social worker or therapist about your feelings. All of your feelings are okay to feel.

- Sometimes, when you have mixed-up feelings, anger or sadness, you can have accidents, like wetting the bed. You could have bad dreams, forget things, or want to run away. When you start feeling safe, some of these accidents stop.

- Tell your foster parents, social worker, or therapist what helps you to feel safe and not afraid.

- Did anyone tell you there are going to be times you miss your parents and times you will be happy not to live where people hurt you? This is okay.

- If you can write, you might want to write down your thoughts and feelings. Writing helps to get feelings out so you can work through them.

- You can also draw pictures that show how you are feeling.

LIFE WITH THE FAMILY I ADOPTED

Every day became easier for me living in my new adoptive home. Most mornings when I wake up, Toby will be sleeping next to me on my soft pillow and red blanket. He needs me in his life. It feels special being needed. In the mornings, we jump up and run to the back door to use the bathroom and play in the pasture. We can smell deer, rabbits, squirrels and birds everywhere. This is perfect for a big dog like me.

I met a new dog friend, Elly, who lives next door and is big like me. Elly is white with black spots. She and I play a game every day. We meet at the fence between our houses. It's a wire fence so we can see and sniff each other. Then, we run up and down on our own side of the long fence barking at each other until we are too tired to run. It's what dogs do to practice protecting their people. We then wag our tails "goodbye" and walk back to our homes. Later, one of us will run to the fence and start barking for the other dog to come out to play. The game starts again. This is so much fun!

Another thing I like is that it is easy to get Momma Donna to rub me behind my ears and kiss the top of my head. I wait until she lies down on the sofa to watch TV. I sneak over and lie down beside her and put my head up on her shoulder. Like I learned from Bear, I look up at her with my sad eyes. She gives in every time! Papa Tony plays ball with me. I help Papa Tony when he is working on the tractor. I guard the tractor to make sure the birds don't sit on it. I will jump up in the air and bark when they come over. It scares them and they fly away. Sometimes, I scare Papa Tony and he jumps and yells, "Shelby!"

Yes, I like it here and I am going to stay.

I still miss my birth family and my foster family. Sometimes my foster family comes out to see us and Kara brings me my favorite snack. I showed Bear how to run the fence but he prefers to sit and watch Elly and me run. When Kara, Haley, and Bear leave, I feel okay because this is my home now and I will see them again. I have a new family and Momma Donna reminded me that I have three families: my birth family, my foster family and my adoptive family. There are lots of people and animals who love me.

WE ADOPT BAC MOOKIE: INTERNATIONAL ADOPTION

One day, Momma Donna and Papa Tony got into their car and left Toby and I to sleep. They always came back and I liked it when they brought us treats. I never knew what they were going to bring back home.

This time, I was lying down in my favorite place on the back porch when Momma Donna and Papa Tony came home.
Toby sniffed, "They have a dog!"
He followed them as they walked to the back porch.

I jumped up when I smelled a dog, too.
"What is that white ball in their arms? It is moving!"

Momma Donna put down the ball.

"Toby and Shelby, we have a new family member. His name is Mookie. He is a puppy. Be nice to him."

Momma Donna called her son, Shane, and I heard her talking to him: "We have a new puppy named Mookie. We were at a High School Fundraiser. An elderly Korean couple was at the Fundraiser carrying a box. Inside the box were three white and furry seven week old puppies.

They looked like snowballs. The couple needed kind people to adopt the puppies because they could not take care of them. It was like an animal international adoption!

"I am usually the first person to fall in love with baby animals. Papa Tony was first this time. He picked up a boy puppy and said, 'Oh, look at this cute little puppy. What kind of dogs are they?'"

She continued, "The couple could not speak English very well. 'You like? He is Jindo. Come from South Korea Island of Jindo. He housebreak himself. No bark unless danger. Very loyal Jindo dog.' I hope Toby and Shelby like him."

Mookie was an active puppy. We all became friends. When I was lying down, he would flop over me and land on the other side of me. Then, he would cuddle up next to me and fall asleep. He was a funny puppy. He thought I was his mother. He jumped all over me and pulled my ears. I held him down with my paw and licked him, just like my doggie mom did to me.

Momma Donna and Papa Tony asked all of their family and friends if they had heard of a Jindo dog. Not even the veterinarian had heard of one. So she searched on the computer and found the Jindo dog website. Everything the Korean couple said was true. He looked just like the puppies on the computer.

Momma Donna wanted to give the puppy a name from his own country. She found out that Koreans put their family name first. The most common family name on the Jindo Island was Bac. We named him Bac Mookie and call him Mookie. She said she wanted to make sure we respected his culture. Jindo dogs are honored as a special dog. There are statues of Jindo dogs in his country. They are great, quick hunters who like to run in packs. They do housebreak themselves and only bark when there is danger. They are loyal to their people families and will never leave them.

Mookie was just a puppy when we adopted him so it was easier for him to learn the rules. We taught him the rules and he trusted us. He did whimper some when he first came to live with us. I knew he missed his doggie mommy and daddy, like I sometimes missed mine.

I told him, "It is okay to whimper. You can cuddle up next to me." I licked his face and he told me his doggie mommy licked his face to make him feel better. Mookie never went to the bathroom in the house. He loves to run and wrestle with me. He leaves Toby alone because Toby is older and doesn't like to wrestle. Mookie and I run around outside hunting for birds, squirrels and rabbits. He is the fastest dog I have ever seen.

He laughs, "Run, Shelby!"

Mookie follows our people around like he is protecting them.

Mookie is older now. He loves that Momma Donna found out information about South Korea, the country his birth family is from. Since there aren't any other Jindo dogs around us, he likes looking at the computer pictures of Jindo dogs. He looks just like the grown up dogs. I laugh because we both have unique positions when lying down. I cross my legs and Mookie puts one leg under his body when he sleeps.

The computer pictures show other Jindo dogs laying the same way. It must be what Jindo dogs do. He wishes he could find his sisters. He knows he looks like them. He is proud to be a Jindo dog just like I am proud to be a Golden Retriever.

Papa Tony said, "We are a colorful family!"

When children are adopted from other countries, it is important that their adoptive family find out everything they can about their birth family and birth country. The best time to find out the heritage of a child is when the adoptive parents are visiting the child's birth country. Adoptive parents need to think of what information their adoptive child may desire throughout their growing years and into their adult years. Children feel loved when adoptive parents respect their birth culture and heritage. This will help the child feel strong and proud. Many adoptive parents practice some of their adoptive children's culture, such as eating foods from their birth country or celebrating holidays of their country.

If you are adopted from another country, this is called International Adoption. Ask your adoptive family about your birth country.

- What is the community and country's culture?
- What are the foods people like to eat?
- What are the customs?
- What are the holidays?
- What are the religions?
- What do people look like there?
  Do you look like the people from your country?
- Are there people from your country living around you?
  Can you meet them so you can identify with someone who is like you?

SHELBY, TOBY AND MOOKIE WITH MOMMA DONNA

WHEN A FRIEND IS GONE: GRIEVING

Friends are fun. My neighbor friend, Elly, and I had fun! We would growl at each other when she walked over to my house or I walked over to her house. The people thought we hated each other. We liked each other but dogs are supposed to protect their property. We practiced acting powerful.

Remember my friend Elly? Our favorite thing to do every day was to bark for each other to come out to the fence between our houses. Then we would bark loudly and run up and down the fence together. When we were tired of running, we would throw our heads up, wag our tails, and walk back home. We called our game "Running the Fence."

One day, Elly did not come to the fence. I barked for her. I knew she wasn't feeling well lately because she could not run far or fast. She tried but she would start coughing. Her people tried to give her some special stuff to make her feel better. They called it medicine.

I waited that day at the fence for her. I sat and sat. Barked and barked. No barks came back from Elly. Momma Donna came out to the fence and petted my head.

"Elly can't run the fence anymore, Shelby. She was so sick her heart stopped beating. She died and went to heaven."

I didn't understand. I went to the fence day after day waiting for Elly.

Weeks went by and then I stopped waiting for her. Sometimes, I still sit by the fence and bark for Elly. It's hard missing her.

Momma Donna said, "You are grieving. Grieving means missing someone you love. When you grieve, you may not want to believe your friend is not going to run the fence anymore. It is okay for you to sit at the fence and wait for her. One day, you will stop waiting at the fence and you will make new friends."

Momma Donna continued talking while hugging me. "When Elly is not there to bark back to you, you may feel angry. You can be angry and be upset with others because your friend left you. You may be sad and want to whimper all day long. All your feelings are okay. You can't help it when your heart is broken."

I am happy Elly was my friend. I will hold on to the fun memories of running the fence. Sometimes, friends or family move away. It hurts then, too. Momma Donna told me that it hurts sometimes when you lose family or friends but love is worth it.

Momma Donna told me, "When someone you love leaves you, it could remind you of when you lost your birth family."

For me, those feelings get mixed up with the new feelings of losing Elly. That helped me understand why I was mad and sad.

As days passed by, I started feeling better. There were days when I was sad and days I laughed and played. I've had a lot of people and animals leave my life. I still try and find some of them. New people and animals will come into my life like Mookie and Toby did. I will find new games to play and I can share my old ones. I won't forget any of my family members and friends. Momma Donna said I can keep them in a special place in my heart and in my Life Book.

For Children:

- *Are there friends, other people or animals you miss?*
- *What are your friends' names?*
- *What fun things did you do together?*
- *Why do you not see them now? It's okay to miss them.*
- *Draw a picture of you and your friend or friends playing.*
- *Do you have photos of you with your friends?*
  Add them to your Life Book.
- *What animals do you miss?*
- *Draw a picture of them or find one on the computer or in a magazine that looks like them. Add them to your Life Book.*

Pages: 165 & 211

LEARNING WHO I AM

My Momma Donna put her arm around me one day while I was sitting by myself on the back porch. Even though I am happy here, there are times when I wonder who I am and where my birth family is living. I wonder if they forgot me. I don't look like any dog around my new land. I guess Momma Donna saw my confusion and sadness.

She hugged me and said, "I have something for you, Shelby."

She didn't have pictures of my birth family so she did her best to help me to know more about myself. She copied pictures of Golden Retriever dogs off the computer, I couldn't believe it! They looked like me! Some had fur lighter than mine and some of the dogs were shorter. The lighter colors and different sizes reminded me of my brother and sisters.

Momma Donna read the information about Golden Retrievers. "You are beautiful and sturdy. Golden Retrievers came from the British Isles."
That sounds far away.

"You are lovable, well-mannered, intelligent dogs with great charm."
I am nice and people like me. Oh, I am feeling better already!

"You are easily trained, always patient and gentle with children."
I love children! Momma Donna and Papa Tony have grandchildren who come over to my house to play. Some of the children dressed me in a tutu so I could

dance with them. We were funny.

"You like to hunt, track, retrieve, perform tricks, and have a great sense of smell. "You are used as therapy dogs, guides for the blind and service dogs for the disabled."

I knew it! I knew we liked to take care of people. I like to smell stuff. We are great dogs. Momma Donna said I was special. She was right.

I wonder if my doggie dad became a police dog and couldn't come home to us because he was catching people who were breaking the law. I bet he is famous. I will look at TV and see if he is on the news. I am very important!

For Children:

- *Do you know where you were born?*
- *What is your heritage?*
- *What is the culture of your family? Are they farmers, artists, factory workers, bankers or inventors?*
- *If you can't find the answers, what would you like your heritage to be?*
- *What other questions do you have?*

TRACKING DOWN MY HISTORY

Now I have lived with my adoptive family for eight years and that is old in dog years. Momma Donna tried for years to find where I was born and find my birth family. Kara helped her by taking her to the place she found me. I would ride with her and try to sniff out my old barn.

Two years ago, we took another road trip. We drove on different roads. I liked to hang my head out the window and smell the wind. I hoped to smell my barn, the berry bushes or my doggie family. Then, one day on one of our trips, I saw her! A Golden Retriever like me was sitting in a yard with a yellow house. I barked and barked!

"Stop, Momma Donna, Stop!"

The other dog barked back at me!

"Okay Shelby! Hold on," yelled Momma Donna.

We stopped. She opened the car door and I ran to the dog! We started sniffing each other!

"Goldie Girl! It's you, Goldie Girl! I have missed you," the girl dog barked. My name! She knew my birth doggie name. I knew her smell but it took me more sniffs to remember. And then I did remember her.

"Sunny! Is this really you?"

Sunny jumped up and down with excitement! She was my big sister, older by five minutes. She didn't look the same. We were puppies when I left home to find food. I asked her about our family. Momma Donna and Papa Tony were sitting on the porch steps of the yellow house talking to Sunny's people. Sunny told me my birth mommy died but she lived a long life with Sunny, Jumper and Barker.

My other sisters lived in the city with other people. She barked for Jumper and Barker to come see me. It was a fun and wild reunion! We jumped and rolled on each other. They all looked like me and smelled like me. Years had passed so we had a lot to catch up on. We promised to stay in touch with each other. I saw Momma Donna and Papa Tony making friends with their people and that made my tail wag. Momma Donna was taking pictures with her camera for my Life Book.

I looked around the land. Then, down the road I saw the giant tree that was next to our barn!

"OUR BARN!" I barked. I took off running towards the tree!

I heard Sunny barking after me to stop!

"No, I have to see our old barn! I miss our old barn!" I barked back. I ran to the tree but I couldn't find the barn.

"Where is my barn?" I ran in circles! I smelled the barn but where was it?

Sunny caught up to me. "A huge storm tore down the barn. I am so sorry, Goldie Girl. We miss it, too."

I whimpered and walked around. I even lay down in a spot where I use to cuddle with my doggie mommy. I put my head down and cried some more.
Sunny sat next to me and licked my face.

"Things change. Animals move and barns fall down. You found us, Goldie Girl. We are together again. We are a family again."
She was right.

Things and people change. We need to hold on to what we do have. My adopted parents helped me find my birth family and where I lived as a puppy. They knew I would appreciate them more if they helped me find my birth family.

Sniff Sniff, what am I smelling? It is very familiar! I stood up and started digging. I couldn't believe it! I saw a piece of leather and I pulled and pulled! Then it popped out of the dirt.

I barked, "My old brown shoe! I found my old brown shoe!"

I jumped up and down carrying my old brown shoe in my mouth! I ran up the road to Sunny's yellow house and up to Momma Donna.

She laughed at me, "Well, I guess you added another shoe to your collection. It sure makes you happy."

If only she could understand doggie talk, she would know I was the happiest dog in the world. I found some of my birth family. I have a caring foster family, a loving adoptive family, and my old brown shoe.

My life has many families with a lot of people and animals who love me. It is different than most of my people and animal friends but that is okay. I like my life because it is **MY LIFE.**

For Children:

- *Can you talk about your birth family with your adoptive parents?*
- *Do you stay in contact with your birth family?*
- *How has your adoptive family helped you find information about your birth family and where you once lived?*
- *What do you know about your birth family now?*
- *Does your adoptive family know you love them more because you can talk about your birth family?*

Have you started filling out your life book pages? Decorate and add some photos and drawings. Get some stickers and use colored pens. Write your life story! Make the book all about YOU.

Thank you for reading my life story and answering my questions. I can't wait to see your Life Book. Look for my other books about going to school and going to the doctor. **I LIKE BEING YOUR FRIEND!**

SHELBY'S LIFE BOOK EXAMPLES

Giving my friend, Peyton, a kiss! The people and animal family and friends have made me happy! I know it is okay to care about a lot of people and animals. I can love my doggie birth family and others, too.

THIS IS ME

My name is: Shelby Foster

I am 5 **years old. My birthday is** May 5th

I am a (boy or girl) girl golden retriever dog

My weight 30 lbs   **My height is** 3'6"

Tape or paste a photo of yourself here. If you don't have one, draw a picture of yourself.

I am special! My people foster and adoptive mothers told me that Golden Retrievers are brave, gentle and beautiful. I love being a Golden Retriever!

WHERE I LIVE NOW

TELL ME ABOUT YOU

I live at: **200 Farm Pond Lane**

Merryville, North Carolina

Draw or put a photo of the house you are living in now.

This is my adoptive home where Momma Donna and Papa Tony live. I like to chase the butterflies that land on the hundreds of flowers. I remember when I came to visit before they adopted me. I liked that I could run and bark everywhere.

My favorite old brown shoe! This was my first toy when I was born. I lost it when I went to live with my foster family but with their help and my adoptive parents, we found my old brown shoe! My families gave me other stuffed animals and I love them for doing that. I like my other toys but nothing can replace my old brown shoe.

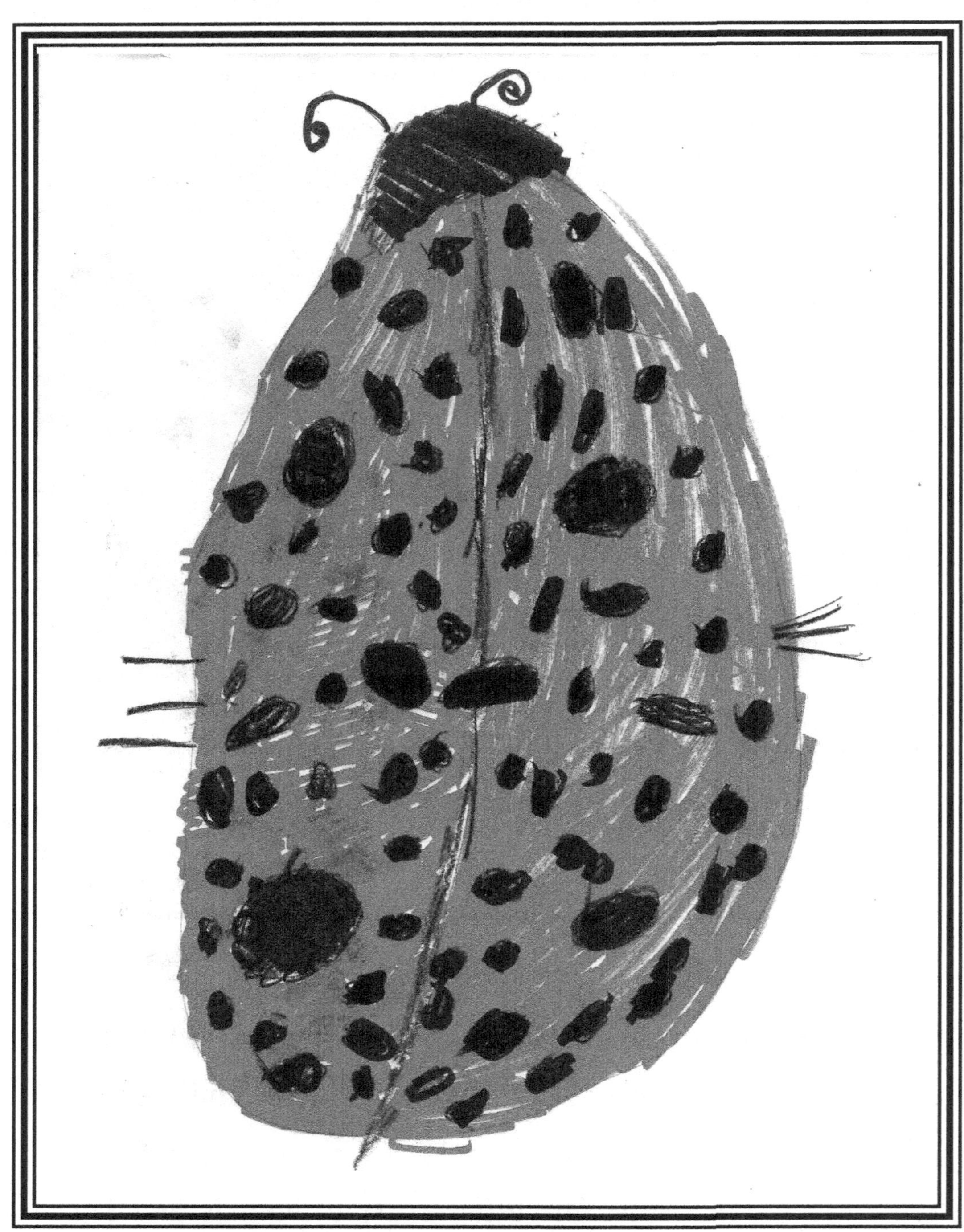

A red ladybug my friend, Brenna, drew just for me. Brenna loves
to pet me and play with me. I like to watch her dance and sing.

~ 2010

Toby and I are eating from our own bowls. I get the big bowl because I am BIG. Toby likes me eating with him. When I went to live with my foster people family, it took me awhile to trust that I would have food every day. I was hungry when I was trying to find food for my birth doggie family. So when my foster people family gave me food I thought it was the last time I would be fed. I hid food under my bed but soon I realized I didn't have to do that. I was fed every day. Toby likes me now. We became friends in my adoptive family. He likes to sleep next to me. He said I protect him. I feel important!

SHELBY AND ME
MY LIFE BOOK

MY NAME ___________________________

Written by Donna H. Foster

Illustrated by Maya Preisler

HI FRIENDS!

These are your Life Book pages. As you read the "Shelby and Me" book, you can fill out the pages about your life. The "Me" in the book is about you so add your name to the front page of your life book. Some of the pages are not about you. For instance; you may be moving back to your birth family so the "Adoption" pages won't be in your Life Book. You may be adopting your foster family or a new family so the "Moving Home" pages won't be about you. Just leave these pages out of your book.

HERE ARE THE STEPS IN MAKING YOUR LIFE BOOK:

- I will share my story through my "Shelby and Me" book. You can share your story by filling out your pages.

- You will find the corresponding life book page number(s) in a box at the bottom of "Shelby and Me" pages. You can read my story and then stop and fill out your life book pages. You can, also, fill out your life book pages any other time. It is up to you.

- Add photos, drawings, stickers to your pages. You can color your life book pages. Be creative! Your life book is yours.

- Put your completed Life Book pages in "page protectors" to keep them safe in your life book binder.

- Keep your pages and other stuff you want to keep in a 3" binder.

- Use colored cardstock paper and glue; add your own artwork, poems, journals, other writings, school work, and collectables (movie tickets, magazine pictures, letters, etc). Have fun capturing your memories and questions!

THIS IS ME

My name is: ____

I am ___________________ years old. **My birthday is** ___________________

I am a (boy or girl) _______________________________________

My weight is ___________________ **My height is** ___________________

Tape or paste a photo of yourself here. If you don't have one, draw a picture of yourself.

WHERE I LIVE NOW

TELL ME ABOUT YOU

I live at: ______________________________

____

Draw or put a photo of the house you are living in now.

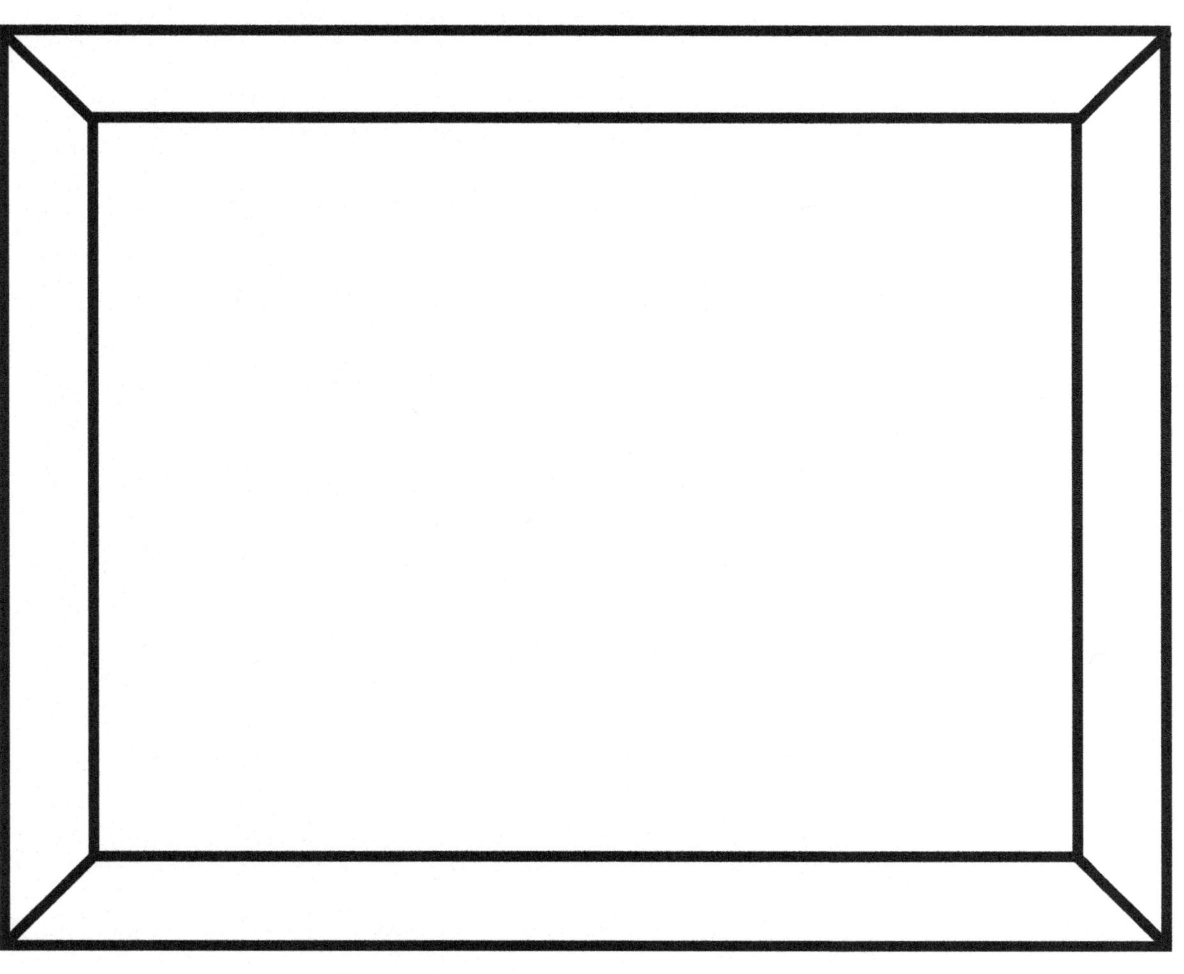

MY FOSTER FAMILY

MY STORY: WHY I CAME INTO FOSTER CARE

WRITE YOUR STORY HERE

(Use more pages if you need more space)

This is why my birth family needed help.

____

____

____

____

____

____

____

I had to live with a family member or foster family because: __________

____

____

____

____

____

The people, pets and places I miss are:

What I need to feel safe:

MY FIRST THOUGHTS AND FEELINGS ABOUT MY FOSTER HOME

When I first saw my foster family's house, I felt: ______________

____

____

When I first met my foster family and their pets, I felt: ______________

____

____

The names and ages of the people in my foster family are: ______________

____

____

I feel most comfortable talking to: ____

____

The pets are: ____

____

My favorite pet(s) is: ____

Because: ____

____

The pets I don't like are: ____

Because: ____

____

The pet I would like is: ____

MY FIRST QUESTIONS ABOUT MY FOSTER FAMILY

When children walk into their new foster home, they have many questions. Sometimes, they are afraid to ask them. Did you have questions? Don't be afraid to ask. Do you know the answers to your questions? Ask your foster parent or social worker.

What rooms am I allowed in? ____________________

____

____

Where do I sleep? ____________________

____

Is anyone sleeping in the room with me? ____________________

____

____

Where do I go to the bathroom? ____________________

____

How do I let the people know I have to go to the bathroom? ________

____

Can I go to the bathroom alone? ____________________

What do I do if I am scared? ____________________

____

Will I get plenty of food here? ______________________

____

What food will I eat here? ______________________

____

What if I don't like the food? ______________________

____

____

Can we play here? ______________________

____

Will I have my own toys? ______________________

____

Where can I play? ______________________

____

Where can I play outside? ______________________

____

Are there any animals living here? ______________________

____

Are they nice or mean? ______________________

____

Are the people nice all of the time? ______________________

____

Will they play with me? _______________________________

How do I know when they like me? _______________________

____

How do I know when they are mad at me? _________________

____

What do they do when they are mad? _____________________

____

Do they hit the children? _______________________________

____

Other questions that I have are: ________________________

____

____

(Write other questions on another piece of paper)

MY DRAWING OR PHOTO OF MY FOSTER HOME:

FUN THINGS TO DO WITH MY FOSTER FAMILY

What my foster family likes to do in their house or out in their yard:

____

____

____

____

____

____

These are my favorite places in the house and yard: _______________

____

____

____

____

I like these favorite places because: _______________________________

____

____

____

____

I have fun with the family because: _______________________________

____

My favorite games to play are: ______________________________

____

____

____

Things I would like to do with my foster family are: ______________

____

____

____

THIS HELPS ME SLEEP

Feeling safe when you sleep is important. Talk to your foster parents about what makes you feel safe.

It helps me go to sleep if: _______________________

____

When I sleep, I like to sleep with a favorite toy, pillow, blanket, music playing, or a fan blowing because: _______________________

____

I brought these things from my home to help me sleep: _______________

____

I like or don't like to have a light on when I go to bed because: _______

____

Things I did not bring with me but wish I had with me: _______________

____

The sounds that scared me are: _______________________

____

The sounds that make me feel safe are: _______________________

____

I like to sleep alone or not alone because: _______________________

____

WHEN DO WE EAT?

When you first came to live with your foster family, did you know you would eat every day? My foster parents helped me to know I would eat every day here by:________________

____

____

My foster family helped me to know when the meals were served.

They are served around:

Breakfast:___________   Lunch:___________   Dinner:___________

My favorite foods are:_______________________

____

____

The foods I do not like are:___________________

____

I like to eat my meals in these rooms:_____________________

____

My special place in the house to eat is:___________________

____

My favorite snacks are:______________________

____

My least favorite snacks are:___________________

NOT ALL BATHROOMS ARE THE SAME

Every person's bathroom is different. Some sinks have two round knobs that turn to start the water. Others have one handle you push up or down. Shower and bathtub faucets can be really confusing. There are rules when you take baths.

The person who showed me the bathroom I could use was: _______________

____

The most confusing things about the sinks, toilet and bathtub were:

____

The rules for the bathroom are (examples: lights off after leaving, you can use the bathroom without asking, close the door for privacy, do not enter the bathroom if someone is in there): _______________________________

____

____

____

What helps me to find the bathroom at night is:_______________________

____

____

What helps me not to be afraid of the bathroom is:___________________

FITTING INTO A NEW FAMILY IS NOT EASY

When you are trying to fit into a new family, it's hard to ask questions or to get the people to understand what you are saying or feeling. When there are other children in the home, it can be fun, but it can be hard, too. Learning how to be friends takes time. Everyone can belong in one house together. Foster parents can love many children. It may take more time for you to care for your foster family. Give yourself time to feel you belong in the new home. Your foster parents want to help you to feel this is your home, too.

The adults or children I found hard to understand me were: ___________

____

We learned how to understand each other by: ___________________________

____

There were times when another child in the foster home was mean to me or

didn't include me when playing. I think it was because: ___________

This made me feel: ____

____

We worked everything out by: _________________________________

____

We still need help with: _______________________________________

UNDERSTANDING FEELINGS: FOSTER HOME

Everyone has feelings: sad, happy, angry, confused, hopeful, hopeless, excited and many more feelings. It is okay to show feelings. Some ways we show feelings can be helpful and some ways can get us into trouble. Talk to your birth parents and/or your foster parents about how to show your feelings. Answer the ways you show your feelings.

HAPPY

How do you show you are happy?

- **Do you laugh out loud?**
- **Do you giggle?**
- **Do you have a big smile on your face?**
- **Do you jump up and down?**

Ways I show I am happy or excited:

____

____

____

____

____

____

____

HOW MY BIRTH PARENTS SHOW HAPPINESS:

- How do your birth parents show happiness?
- What makes them happy?
- How do you know when they are happy?

Ways my birth family express happiness: _______________________

____

____

____

____

____

____

____

HOW MY FOSTER PARENTS SHOW HAPPINESS:

Ask your foster parents how you will know when they are happy.

- How do the other family members show happiness?
- What makes them happy?

Ways my foster family express happiness: _______________________

____

____

____

____

SADNESS

- How do you show you are sad?
- Do you cry?
- Do you crawl up in a ball on the bed?
- Do you tell someone you are sad?
- Do you tell everyone to leave you alone?
- Do you want someone to hold you?

Ways I show I am sad: ________________________

____

____

____

____

____

HOW MY BIRTH PARENTS SHOW SADNESS:

- How do your birth parents show sadness?
- What makes them sad?
- How do you know when they are sad?
- What did your birth family want you to do when they were sad?

Ways my birth family express sadness: ________________________

____

____

____

____

HOW MY FOSTER PARENTS SHOW SADNESS:

Ask your foster parents how you will know when they are sad.

- How do the other family members show sadness?
- What makes them sad?
- What do they want you to do if they are sad?

Ways my foster family express sadness: ___________________________

____

____

____

____

____

____

____

____

ANGER

How do you show you are mad or angry?

- **Do you yell?**
- **Do you throw things?**
- **Do you break things?**
- **Do you run?**
- **Do you tell someone you are mad?**
- **Do you hide your anger?**
- **Do you cry?**
- **Do you want to be left alone?**
- **Do you hit things?**
- **Do you hit people or animals?**

Ways I show my anger: _______________________

____

____

Things that make me angry: _______________________

____

HOW MY BIRTH PARENTS SHOW ANGER:

- **How do your birth parents show anger?**
- **What makes them angry?**
- **How do you know when they are angry?**

Ways my birth family express anger: _______________________

____

HOW MY FOSTER PARENTS SHOW ANGER:

Ask your foster parents how you will know when they are angry.

- How do the other family members show anger?
- What makes them angry?
- What do they want you to do if they are angry?
- Will they still like you if they are angry at you?

Ways my foster family express anger: _______________________

____

____

____

____

____

My foster parents helped me to understand okay ways to show my anger.

Some of the ways are: _______________________________________

____

____

____

____

MY BIRTH FAMILY

VISITS WITH MY BIRTH FAMILY

Visiting your birth family can be exciting, sad and scary. It is not your fault that you are in foster care. Your family wants to see you. They want to see that you are safe, happy and that you still love them. Your foster parents and social worker want to make sure you are ready for your visits. Your birth parents might be upset because you are not home with them. They may say things that make you sad. There are big people helping your family. You might have questions about your birth family.

When can I visit with my parents? _______________________________________

____

Will my brothers and sisters be there? __________________________________

____

When can I visit my grandparents, aunts, uncles and cousins? ____________

____

Where are the visits going to be? _______________________________________

____

Can I bring something to give to them; like a picture I drew or pictures

 of me? ____

____

Can I take photos with a camera during a visit? _________________________

____

Can I bring a picnic or snacks to share with my family? I would like

to bring: ____

Can they bring me some of my favorite things from home?_______________

I would like for them to bring me:_______________________________

____

____

____

Where do I go after the visit? _____________________________________

____

What questions do you have for your social worker?__________________

____

____

____

____

____

____

____

When can I go home?____

____

____

____

MY BIRTH INFORMATION

This is about you when you were a little baby. If you don't know the information, you can guess the answer. You may say, "I think I weighed 7 pounds when I was born." Later, if you find out the real information, you can change what you wrote. If you don't have photos of yourself, cut some pictures out of magazines that look like you or the people in your family.

My full name is:____

My birthday is:____

The hospital I was born in:______________________________________

I was born in the city of:_______________________________________

I weighed_______.lbs. _______ oz.   I was_______________in. long.

When I was born, the people that were there:_______________________

____

The persons I look like are:_____________________________________

____

MY BABY PICTURE

MY BIRTH MOTHER

MOTHER'S NAME: _______________________________

Mother's birth date: _______________________________

Mother's eye color: _______________________________

Hair color: _______________________________

Her mother's name: _______________________________

Her father's name: _______________________________

Her siblings' names: _______________________________

Where my mother grew up: _______________________________

Where my mother lives: _______________________________

Schools my mother attended: _______________________________

Hobbies my mother likes to do: _______________________________

Mother's likes and dislikes: _______________________________

Photo of my mother or a picture of what she looks like:

MY BIRTH FATHER

FATHER'S NAME:_______________________________

Father's birth date:_______________________________

Father's eye color:_______________________________

Hair color:_______________________________

His mother's name:_______________________________

His father's name:_______________________________

His siblings' names:_______________________________

Where my Father grew up:_______________________________

Where my Father lives:_______________________________

Schools my Father attended:_______________________________

Hobbies my Father likes to do:_______________________________

Father's likes and dislikes:_______________________________

Photo of my Father or a picture of what he looks like:

MY BIRTH SIBLINGS

MY BROTHERS AND SISTERS

Sister's or Brother's name:_______________________________________

Sister's or Brother's birth date:_________________________________

Special qualities:____

____

____

Sister's or Brother's name:_______________________________________

Sister's or Brother's birth date:_________________________________

Special qualities:____

____

____

Sister's or Brother's name:_______________________________________

Sister's or Brother's birth date:_________________________________

Special qualities:____

____

____

If you have more than three siblings, write them on a separate piece of paper. On separate pages add photos of you with your siblings. Write some of your favorite memories.

BIRTH FAMILY MEDICAL INFORMATION

ALL ABOUT ME

I think my "firsts" happened during these times. If I don't know some of my firsts, I will write "I think" this is when or what I did. If I know my firsts, I will write I "did" this or that.

I first smiled:_______________________________

I first held my head up:_______________________

I first cut a tooth:___________________________

I first sat up:________________________________

My first word was:____________________________

I first crawled:_______________________________

I first walked:________________________________

My favorite baby toy:_________________________________

My other baby favorites were:_________________________

My first riding toy was:______________________________

I learned to ride a bicycle when I was:_______________

Other firsts:____

____

____

____

____

____

GETTING TO KNOW ME

My favorite games to play indoors are:_______________________________

My favorite games to play outdoors are:_______________________________

I am good at: _______________________________

I am not good at:_______________________________

My favorite foods are:_______________________________

My least favorite foods are:_______________________________

Other things that are special about me:_______________________________

____

____

My friends' names are: _______________________________

____

____

____

FRIENDS I MISS

Name of friend:_______________________________

Where did you both live?_______________________________

____

What was special about your friend?_______________________________

____

What did you like to do together?_______________________________

____

Do you see your friend now?_______________________________

Address & phone number:_______________________________

____

Name of friend:_______________________________

Where did you both live?_______________________________

What was special about your friend?_______________________________

____

What did you like to do together?_______________________________

____

Do you see your friend now?_______________________________

Address & phone number:_______________________________

____

Name of friend:_______________________________

Where did you both live? _______________________________________

What was special about your friend? _______________________________

____

What did you like to do together? __________________________________

____

Do you see your friend now? _______________________________________

Address & phone number: ____

____

Name of friend: ____

Where did you both live? ____

What was special about your friend? _________________________________

____

What did you like to do together? ___________________

____

Do you see your friend now? ________________________

List on another page teachers and others you miss.

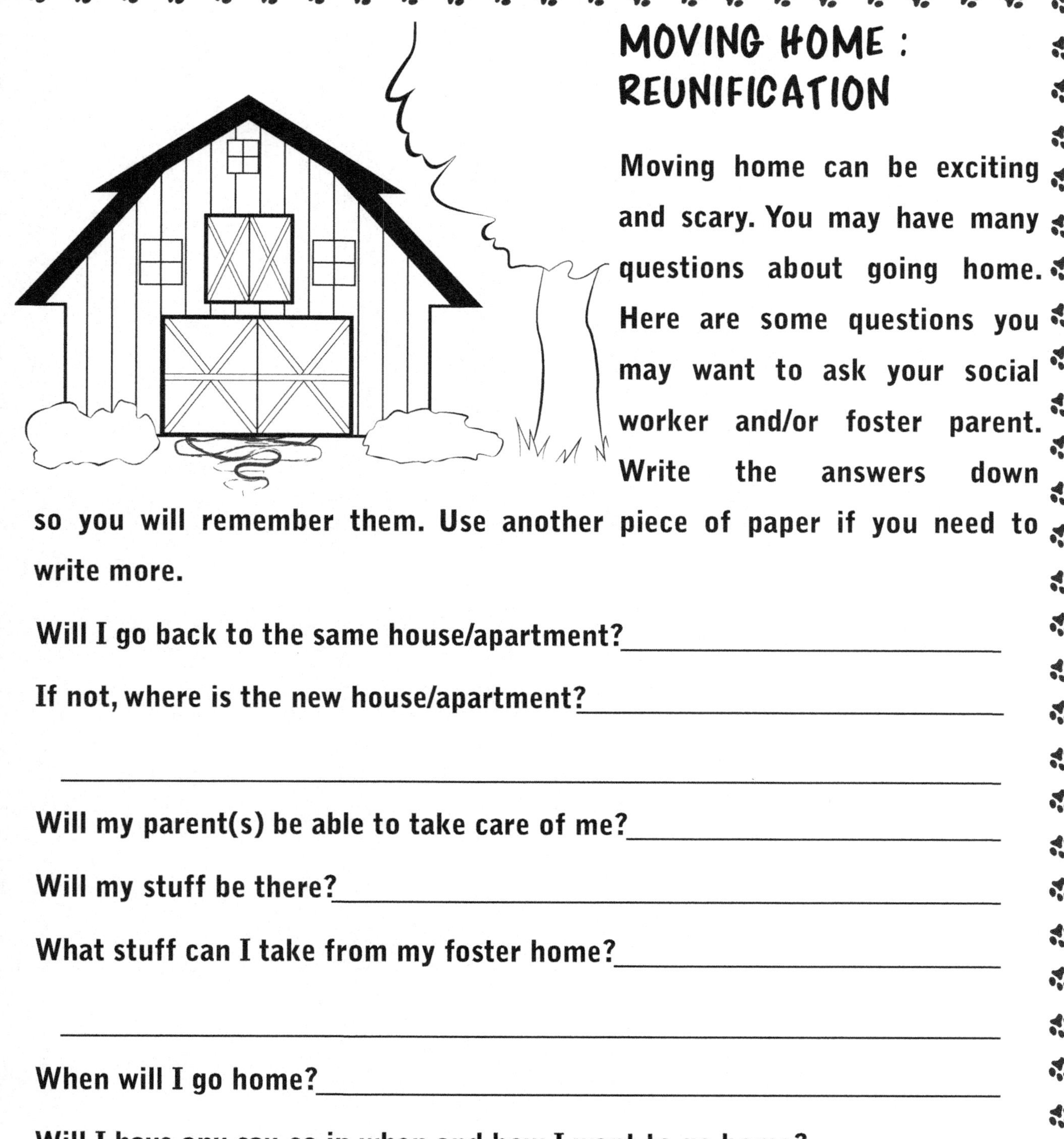

MOVING HOME: REUNIFICATION

Moving home can be exciting and scary. You may have many questions about going home. Here are some questions you may want to ask your social worker and/or foster parent. Write the answers down so you will remember them. Use another piece of paper if you need to write more.

Will I go back to the same house/apartment?______________________

If not, where is the new house/apartment?______________________

____

Will my parent(s) be able to take care of me?______________________

Will my stuff be there?______________________

What stuff can I take from my foster home?______________________

____

When will I go home?______________________

Will I have any say-so in when and how I want to go home?______________________

These are the people I want to help me go home:______________________

____

____

Can I go home slowly starting with visits then add more days at home?____

____

After I go home, will I be able to see my foster family?________________

After I go home, will I be able to see my friends and teachers?__________

____

These are the people I want to see: ____________________________________

____

Other questions:____

____

____

____

____

____

____

____

____

____

____

____

____

MY ADOPTIVE FAMILY

MY ADOPTION STORY

MY ADOPTED NAME: _______________________

____

DATE OF ADOPTION: _______________________

____

MY ADOPTED PARENTS ARE: _______________

____

MY ADOPTED BROTHERS AND SISTERS:_______________

____

____

____

____

____

____

____

____

____

MY FIRST THOUGHTS AND FEELINGS ABOUT MY ADOPTIVE HOME

When I first saw my adoptive family's house, I felt: _______________

____

____

When I first met my adoptive family and their pets, I felt: _______________

____

____

The names and ages of the people in my adoptive family are: _______________

____

____

I feel most comfortable talking to: _______________________________

____

The pets are: _______________________________________

____

My favorite pet(s) are: _________________________________

____

Because: ____________________________

The pets I don't like are: _________________________

Because: ____________________________

____

The pet I would like is: _________________________

MY FIRST QUESTIONS ABOUT MY ADOPTED FAMILY

When children walk into their new adopted home, they have many questions. Your adoptive family may be different from your birth or foster family. Sometimes, children are afraid to ask their adoptive parents questions. Did you have any questions? Don't be afraid to ask questions.

What rooms am I allowed in?_______________________________

____

____

Where do I sleep?____

____

Is anyone sleeping in the room with me?____________________

____

____

Where do I go to the bathroom?____________________________

____

How do I let the people know I have to go to the bathroom?______

____

Can I go to the bathroom alone?___________________________

What do I do if I am scared?

____

Will I get plenty of food here?

What food will I eat here?

What if I don't like the food?

Can we play here?

Will I have my own toys?

Where can I play?

Where can I play outside?

Are there any animals living here?

Are they nice or mean?

Are the people nice all of the time?

Will they play with me?_______________________________________

How do I know when they like me?_______________________________

____

How do I know when they are mad at me?_________________________

____

What do they do when they are mad?_____________________________

____

Do they hit the children?______________________________________

____

Other questions that I have are: _______________________________

____

____

(Write other questions on another piece of paper)

MY DRAWING OR PHOTO OF MY ADOPTED HOME:

FUN THINGS TO DO WITH MY ADOPTED FAMILY

What fun things my adopted family likes to do at their house or in their yard: ____________

____

____

____

____

These are my favorite places in the house and yard: ____________

____

____

____

I like these favorite places because: ____________

____

____

____

I have fun with the family because: ____________

____

____

My favorite games to play are:

Things I would like to do with my adoptive family are:

THIS HELPS ME SLEEP

Feeling safe when you sleep is important. Talk to your adoptive parents about what makes you feel safe.

It helps me go to sleep if:

____

When I sleep, I like to sleep with a favorite toy, pillow, blanket, music playing, or a fan blowing because:_______________________________

____

I brought these things from my home to help me sleep:_______________

____

I like or don't like to have a light on when I go to bed because:_________

____

Things I did not bring with me but wish I had with me:_______________

____

The sounds that scared me are:_________________________________

____

The sounds that make me feel safe are:__________________________

____

I like to sleep alone or not alone because:________________________

____

WHEN DO WE EAT?

When you first came to live with your adoptive
family, did you know you would eat every day?
My adoptive parents helped me to know I would
eat every day here by:_______________________________

____

____

My adoptive family helped me to know when the meals were served.

They are served around:

Breakfast:____________   Lunch:____________   Dinner:____________

My favorite foods are:_______________________________

____

____

The foods I do not like are:_______________________________

____

I like to eat my meals in these rooms:_______________________________

____

My special place in the house to eat is:_______________________________

____

My favorite snacks are:_______________________________

____

My least favorite snacks are:_______________________________

NOT ALL BATHROOMS ARE THE SAME

Every person's bathroom is different. Some sinks have two round knobs that turn to start the water. Others have one handle you push up or down. Shower and bathtub faucets can be really confusing. There are rules when you take baths.

The person who showed me the bathroom I could use was:_______________

____

The most confusing things about the sinks, toilet and bathtub were:

____

____

The rules for the bathroom are (examples: lights off after leaving, you can use the bathroom without asking, close the door for privacy, do not enter the bathroom if someone is in there):_______________

____

____

____

What helps me to find the bathroom at night is:

____

What helps me not to be afraid of the

bathroom is:_______________________________________

____

FITTING INTO AN ADOPTIVE FAMILY IS NOT EASY

When you are trying to fit into a new family, it's hard to ask questions or to get the people to understand what you are saying or feeling. When there are other children in the home, it can be fun, but it can be difficult, too. Learning how to be friends takes time. Everyone can belong in one house together. Parents can love many children. It may take more time for you to care for your new family. Give yourself time to feel you belong in the new home. Your adoptive family wants to help you to feel this is your home, too.

I found it difficult getting the adults to understand me when:_____________

____

____

We learned how to understand each other by:_____________________________

____

____

There were times when another child in the adopted home was mean to me or didn't include me when playing. I think it was because:_____________

____

____

This made me feel:____

____

____

We worked everything out by:_______________________________________

____

UNDERSTANDING FEELINGS : ADOPTION

Everyone has feelings: sad, happy, angry, confused, hopeful, hopeless, excited and many more feelings. It is okay to show feelings. Some ways we show feelings can be helpful and some ways can get us into trouble. Talk to your adoptive parents about how to show your feelings. Answer the ways you show your feelings.

HAPPY

How do you show you are happy?

- Do you laugh out loud?
- Do you giggle?
- Do you have a big smile on your face?
- Do you jump up and down?

Ways I show I am happy or excited:_____________

____

____

____

____

Things that make me happy:_____________________

____

____

____

____

HOW MY BIRTH PARENTS SHOW HAPPINESS:

- How do your birth parents show happiness?
- What makes them happy?
- How do you know when they are happy?

Ways my birth family shows happiness:_______

____

____

____

HOW MY FOSTER PARENTS SHOW HAPPINESS:

Ask your foster parents how you will know when they are happy.

- How do the other family members show happiness?
- What makes them happy?

Ways my foster family express happiness:_______________________

____

____

____

HOW MY ADOPTIVE PARENTS SHOW HAPPINESS:

Ask your foster parents how you will know when they are happy.

- How do the other family members show happy?
- What makes them happy?

Ways my adoptive family express happiness:_______________________

____

SADNESS

How do you show you are sad?

- Do you cry?

- Do you crawl up in a ball on the bed?

- Do you tell someone you are sad?

- Do you tell everyone to leave you alone?

- Do you want someone to hold you?

Ways I show I am sad: _______________________

____

____

____

Things that make me sad: _____________________

____

____

____

HOW MY BIRTH PARENTS SHOW SADNESS:

- How do your birth parents show sadness?

- What makes them sad?

- How do you know when they are sad?

- What did your birth family want you to do when they were sad?

Ways my birth family express sadness: ___________

____

____

HOW MY FOSTER PARENTS SHOW SADNESS:

Ask your foster parents how you will know when they are sad.

- How do the other family members show sadness?
- What makes them sad?
- What do they want you to do if they are sad?

Ways my foster family express sadness:

____

____

____

____

____

HOW MY ADOPTIVE PARENTS SHOW SADNESS:

Ask your foster parents how you will know when they are sad.

- How do the other family members show anger?
- What makes them sad?
- What do they want you to do if they are sad?

Ways my adoptive family express sadness:______________________

____

____

____

____

ANGER

How do you show you are mad or angry?

- Do you yell?
- Do you throw things?
- Do you break things?
- Do you run?
- Do you tell someone you are mad?
- Do you hide your anger?
- Do you cry?
- Do you want to be left alone?
- Do you hit things?
- Do you hit people or animals?

Ways I show my anger:_______________________________

____

____

What makes me angry:_______________________________

____

____

HOW MY BIRTH PARENTS SHOW ANGER:

- How do your birth parents show anger?
- What makes them angry?
- How do you know when they are angry?

Ways my birth family express anger:_______________________

____

HOW MY FOSTER PARENTS SHOW ANGER:

Ask your foster parents how you will know when they are angry.

- How do the other family members show anger?
- What makes them angry?
- What do they want you to do if they are angry?
- Will they still like you if they are angry at you?

Ways my foster family express anger:________________________________

____

____

____

____

____

HOW MY ADOPTIVE PARENTS SHOW ANGER:

Ask your foster parents how you will know when they are angry.

- How do the other family members show anger?
- What makes them angry?
- What do they want you to do if they are angry?
- Will they still like you if they are angry at you?

Ways my adoptive family shows anger:________________________________

____

____

____

My adoptive parents helped me to know the okay ways I can show my anger.

Here are some of the ways: _______________________________________

____

____

____

____

____

____

It is very important to know your feelings may be mixed up sometimes. All of your feelings are okay to have. Your adoptive parents may have other people to help you with your feelings. They are there to help you. Talk to your adoptive parents about how you feel.

Name of friend:

Where did you both live?

What was special about your friend?

What did you like to do together?

Do you see your friend now?

Address & phone number:

Name of friend:

Where did you both live?

What was special about your friend?

What did you like to do together?

Do you see your friend now?

Address & phone number:

Name of friend:

Where did you both live?____

____

What was special about your friend?__________________________________

____

What did you like to do together?____________________________________

____

Do you see your friend now?____

Address & phone number:____

____

Name of friend:____

Where did you both live?____________________

____

What was special about your friend?________

____

What did you like to do together?__________

____

Do you see your friend now?__________

List on another page teachers and others
you miss.

SPECIAL MEMORIES

SCHOOL PICTURE

SCHOOL MEMORIES

SCHOOL PICTURE
SCHOOL MEMORIES

SCHOOL PICTURE

SCHOOL MEMORIES

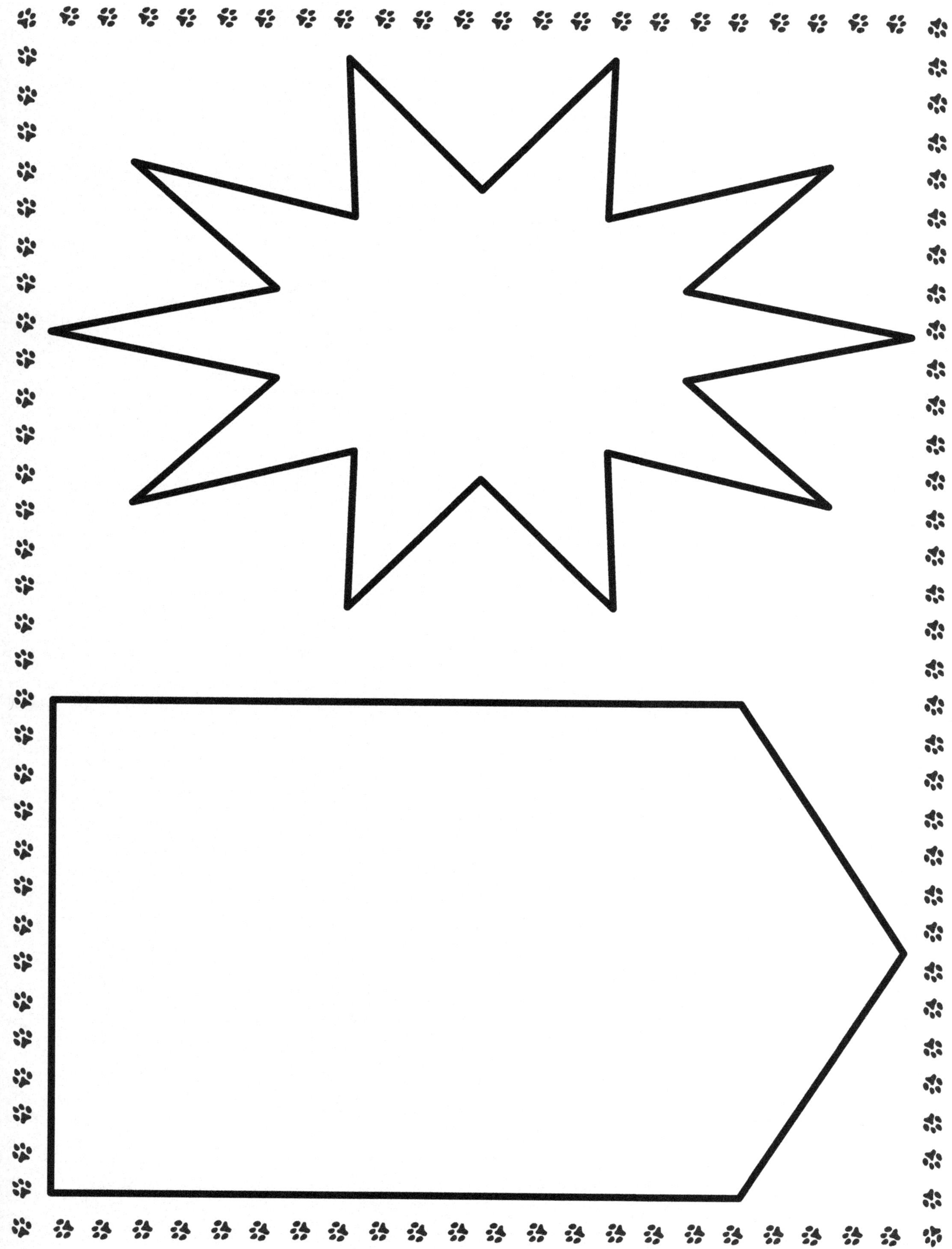

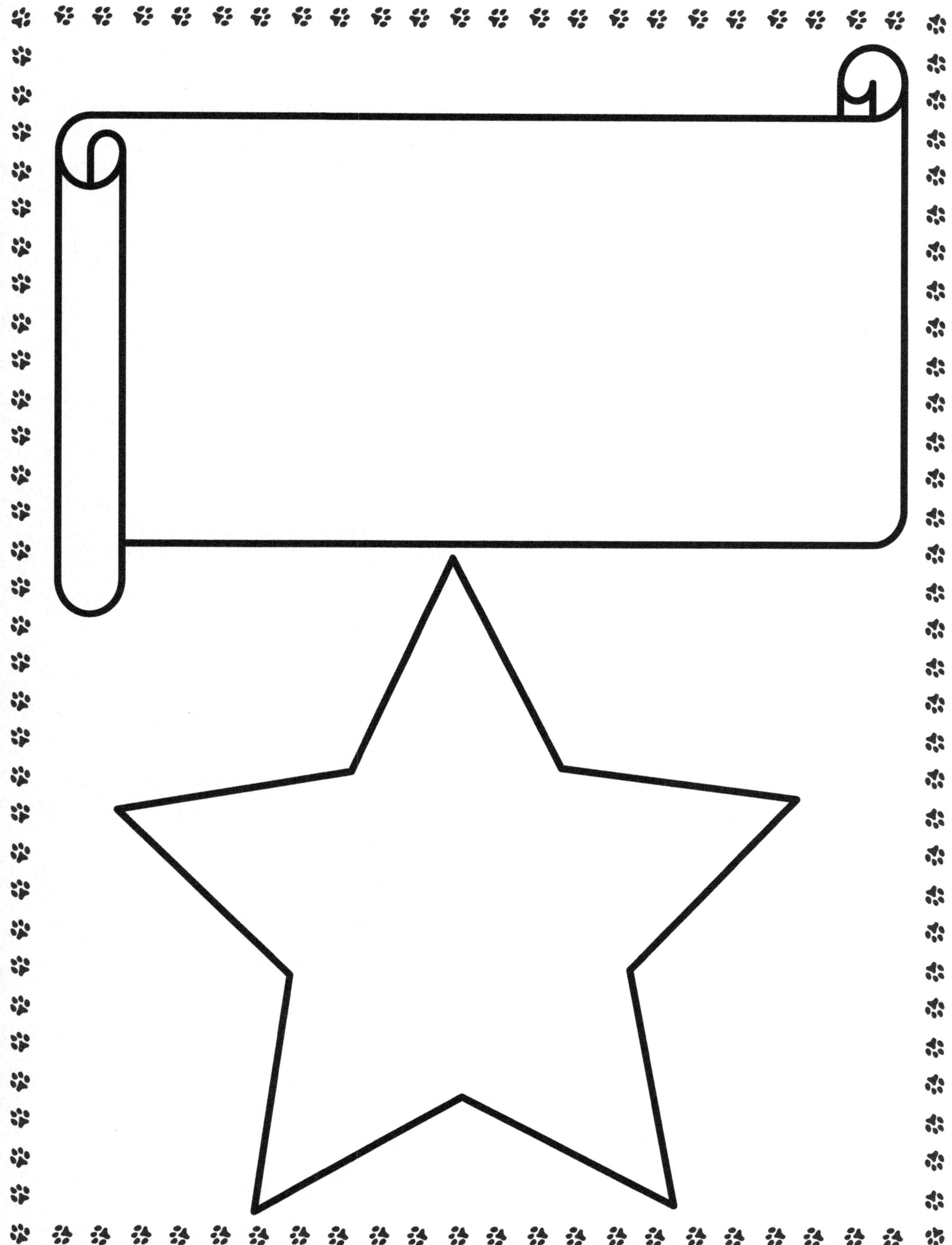

I AM A STAR

I like to do....   My talents are...   I am special because...

Write them or draw them in the stars!

MY MEDICAL INFORMATION

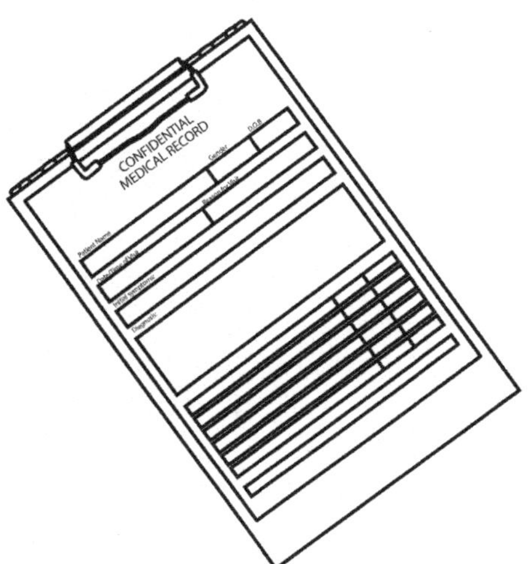

MY BIRTHDAY

Date: _____________ Age: _____________

Celebrated at: _____________

The people who celebrated with me were: _____________

____

____

This is how I celebrated my birthday: _____________

____

____

MY BIRTHDAY

Date: _____________________ **Age:** _____________________

Celebrated at: _____________________

The people who celebrated with me were: _____________________

____

____

This is how I celebrated my birthday: _____________________

____

____

MY BIRTHDAY

Date: _______________ **Age:** _______________

Celebrated at: _______________________________

The people who celebrated with me were: _______________

____

____

This is how I celebrated my birthday: _______________

____

____

HOLIDAYS

A special holiday is: _______________________

Date: _______________________

I celebrated by: _______________________

____

____

____

HOLIDAYS

A special holiday is: _______________________________

Date: ____

I celebrated by: ____________________________________

____

____

____

HOLIDAYS

A special holiday is: _______________________________

Date: _______________________________

I celebrated by: _______________________________

____

____

____

BELIEFS

My birth family believes in: _______________________

____

____

I believe in: _______________________________

____

____

How I like to practice my beliefs: ___________________

____

____

____

____

____

____

WHEN I GROW UP...

I want to live:____________________________________

____

____

____

The job I want is: _________________________________

____

____

____

Other important things I want when I grow up:___________

____

____

____

____

MY TREASURES

My stuff is important to me. Here is some of the stuff I want to keep. I can put some of my stuff in a special keepsake box.

MY TREASURES

My stuff is important to me. Here is some of the stuff I want to keep. I can put some of my stuff in a special keepsake box.

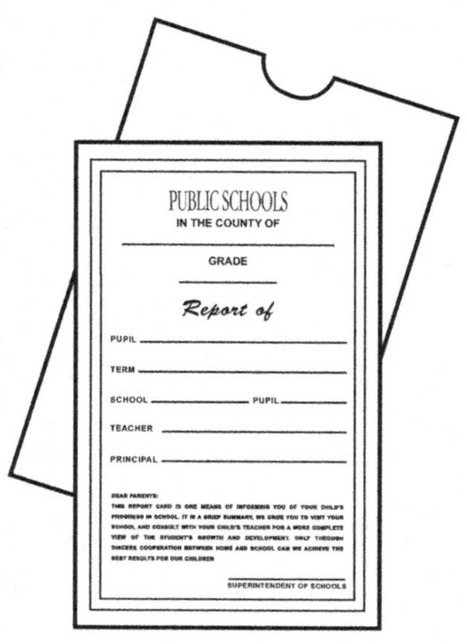

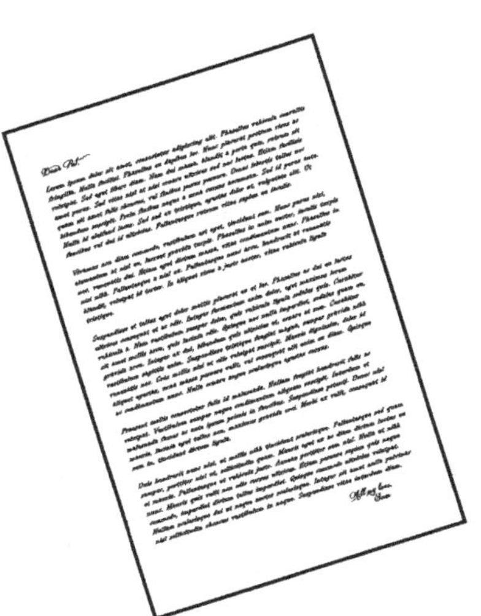

MY TREASURES

My stuff is important to me. Here is some of the stuff I want to keep. I can put some of my stuff in a special keepsake box.

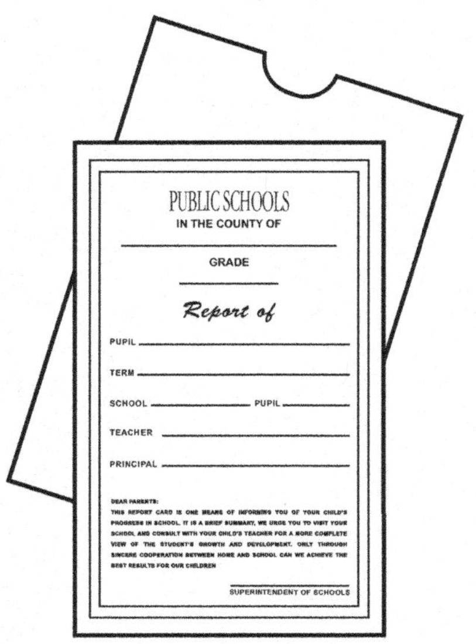

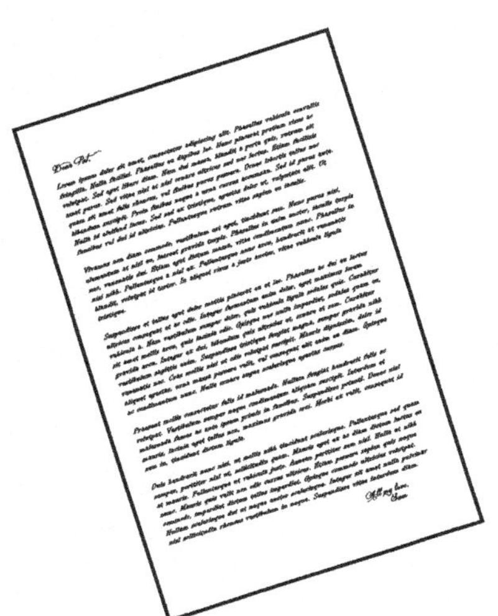

Made in the USA
Monee, IL
16 May 2021